THE SECRET OF
THE EMPIRE

THE SECRET OF THE EMPIRE
A King Montezuma Story

Book 2

Keith H. Adkins

ISBN-13: 9798989577644
Printed in the United States of America
ChrisJen Publications
www.keithhadkins.com
Cover design by: ebooklaunch.com

Contents

ACT I
Before the Exile

ACT II
The Fall of the Empires

ACT III
During the Exile

ACT IV
After the Exile

INTRODUCTION
A Mesoamerica Timeline

The Formative Period (1500 B.C.–A.D. 300)

The Olmec Civilization flourished from 1200–400 B.C., centered near modern-day Veracruz, and reaching as far south as present-day Nicaragua. They also had an extensive trade network, as Guatemalan jade artifacts have been found in Olmec sites.

The Maya Civilization flourished from 1000 B.C.-A.D. 1521 They developed a writing system, produced beautiful art and created a calendar system. The ruins of their pyramids can be found all over the Yucatan Peninsula, including Chichen Itza and Tulum.

The Zapotec Civilization flourished from 500 B.C.–A.D. 1000, centered near modern-day Oaxaca. They established trade links with the Olmecs, and had a sophisticated knowledge of engineering. They had a highly organized governance system, and developed the predecessor to the Maya and Aztec calendars.

The Classic Period (A.D. 300 – 950)
The Teotihuacan Civilization flourished from A.D. 1-650

and was one of the largest cities in the world. Monuments found there, with hieroglyphic texts, describe its divine origins, in a societal transformation from shamans to kings.

The Tajin civilization flourished from A.D. 550-1100. Located near Veracruz, this was a ceremonial center renowned for outstanding artistic developments in intricate mosaic stone facades and colorful fresco painting.

The Postclassic Period (A.D. 950 – 1521)

The Mixtec Civilization flourished from A.D. 900-1521. Their craftspeople used exotic materials of gold, silver, and copper from Central and South America, while turquoise from the American southwest was exchanged for the plumage of Scarlet Macaws.

The Aztec Civilization flourished from A.D. 1200-1521. Spanish conquistadors, led by Hernán Cortés, overthrew the Aztec Empire and captured Tenochtitlan. The Aztec or Mexica people gave their name to the nation of Mexico, while their city of Tenochtitlan became what we know as Mexico City.

PREFACE
A Border Crossing

The front door suddenly swung open, and there stood our son Jameson, fresh home from his first year of college. "Long time, no see!" I said with my usual silly flair. "Dad! Arizona State is only a few miles away," Jameson volleyed back in his equally teasing way. He really was a chip off the old block, so it was good to have him home for the summer. He was serious about staying away most of his first year, so he could focus on his studies, but we at least kept in touch every week. We were quite close, though truth be known, he was closer to his mother. The Mexican culture puts family first, and I often put wo rk first.

"Hijo!" screamed his mother, as she came running to greet him. I could see tears falling from her eyes as they hugged, and it rather choked me up, too. Soon we settled into the kitchen and chatted while she cooked some tortillas on the placa. The aroma immediately got the hunger pangs stirring, so we nibbled on some fresh fruit and Oaxaca cheese. Mom learned her cooking skills from her mother, and Jameson was so spoiled on his mother's food that he hated all the Mexican restaurants in town. He always said that nothing compared to Mom's food. When dinner was served, the conversation steered toward Jameson and he excitedly shared about his most recent class.

The religion course was livelier than I could have expected, after touring Mexico with you last summer, Dad." It did my heart good to know it had been worthwhile. It was his eighteenth birthday present from me and his mother, and we all knew it was as much for me as it was for him. "The class was 'The Pentateuch and the Deuteronomistic History,' and everything

The Secret of the Empire

the professor talked about became more than words on paper. I couldn't believe how powerfully the stories came alive from having been there. I could see the sights, and hear the sounds, and smell the aromas as the text was discussed.

"Anyway, I was thinking." About that time his mother folded her arms and had a small scowl on her face. She usually was one step ahead of us, and once again she was right. "To begin my second year of college, I would love to take a class on the Prophecies of the Shamans. So, if there is any chance at all, I would love to return to Mexico this summer with you, Dad, and experience the context of those books."

Mom unfolded her arms and surprised us by saying, "Only if I can join you."

Jameson and I looked at each other and were beyond delighted, so I said, "Let me think about how we might make this thing happen, not to mention the cost involved." As a High School history teacher in the inner city of Phoenix, I never made much money, but had the summers off. My wife is a Social Worker for the Poor People's Campaign, and both of our jobs were influenced by the ethical teachings of Jim Caldwell.

As I prepared for the trip, I made a phone call to Geraldo, the tour guide from last year's trip. He couldn't help us because he recently broke his foot in a farming mishap, but he gave me some great advice. When I told him what we wanted to do, he said, "The shamans prophesied from Tenochtitlan in the Southern Empire, and Monterrey in the Northern Empire. Since you've been to Tenochtitlan, you can talk about those prophecies without returning there, so I would recommend traveling to Monterrey and sharing from that context."

Geraldo had been a great asset, so I really had to think about a trip without him. I was quite familiar with the prophecies, so I decided to spend some time at the library and polish up on my understandings. When I told Jameson the news about Geraldo, and that I was planning on being the guide this time, he said, "Dad, you don't look Mexican enough." His wry smile set me at ease that he was happy with the plan, and having his mother with us would be a wonderful benefit in many ways. After thinking about the cost, I decided to drive there and see if we could keep the trip down to two weeks or less.

My wife had plenty of paid time off piled up, so she put in her request for some vacation time and got approved. We spent the next several days packing and buying a few snack items. Well, actually, I used that time to do a little more study at the library. My wife seems to think that I always have something to do instead of help with chores. Soon after we were married, I did some laundry and ruined her expensive cashmere sweater, which resulted in my being banned from doing laundry. I also cooked her an omelette one morning and creatively added vanilla extract, resulting in my being expelled from cooking duties. One can always hope for more disqualifications.

We packed the car and headed out early the following morning. We had a nineteen-hour drive ahead of us, so we planned to get halfway on the first day, stopping at Fort Stockton, Texas.

"So, what way are we going, Dad?" Jameson inquired from the back seat.

"Thought we'd take I-10 all the way to Fort Stockton."

Jameson quickly pulled out his phone and opened the 'maps' ap. "So, we won't be doing the border crossing at El Paso?"

"No. I've always wanted to see southern Texas."

"So, are we going to cross at Ciudad Acuña?"

The Secret of the Empire

"No, again. I want to follow along the Rio Grande, then cross the border at Laredo, Texas." Jameson seemed content with the plan, so he settled in to enjoy his phone as we first headed to Tucson. I glanced over at my wife in the passenger seat, and my heart was full, because I was so happy to have her join us. Her given name is Solana, meaning sunshine, but she always went by 'Sol.' She certainly was my heart and soul, and we did some enjoyable reminiscing as we traveled through southeastern Arizona.

When we passed by the turn to Tombstone, she said, "Remember that family trip to see some of the history from our Caldwellian faith?"

"I do," said a cheery Jameson. "Pretty cool to see where Wyatt Earp and Doc Holliday took on the Clanton Gang at the O.K. Corral. Was that before Wyatt was called up to Phoenix to arrest Jim Caldwell or after?"

"After," Sol and I said in harmony.

"On that trip," said Sol, "we also visited the little mining town of Bisbee. That's where my ancestors arrived in the United States to work the copper mines, after leaving Oaxaca, Mexico."

"I loved the train ride into the Copper Queen Mine," said Jameson. "I can't believe they used to mine by candlelight!"

"They were a hearty group, for sure," I said. Before long we crossed the state line into New Mexico and finally stopped in El Paso for lunch. We wanted some Mexican food and hoped that being so close to Mexico we might find something good. We passed dozens of possibilities on the I-10 corridor through the middle of the city, but finally chose Taquizas Los Pistoleros. We discovered that if you pull up to a restaurant, and find all out of license plates on the cars are out of state, you should just keep going. But if you find all local plates, the food will probably be good. Something seemed strange when we stopped, then Jameson laughed and announced that it was a catering service only.

Not just a little bit frustrated, we continued, and next found Julio's Mexican Food. Couldn't possibly be as good as Sol's, but we were hungry and ready to eat. The menu looked great, so we were hopeful. I ordered Chicken Tampiquena, Sol ordered Chiles Rellenos, and Jameson ordered Julio's Mexican Plate. When the food came out, Sol did her usual thing of spreading the food around and lightly sampling from the interior. To our great surprise, she smiled and said, "Not bad." Don't get me wrong, that in no way implies it was good. It just meant that it was edible. Meanwhile, Jameson and I loved our orders.

After leaving El Paso, the interstate paralleled the Rio Grande for a while, then turned east. Fort Stockton didn't come soon enough, because we were getting tired of traveling, and checked into the Fairfield Inn & Suites. Since Fort Stockton was a small town, the prices were very reasonable, and the accommodations were pleasant. We like staying at the Marriott Bonvoy brand of hotels when traveling, and when one is available. In the morning, we enjoyed the free hot breakfast buffet, then checked out and loaded up the car. Jameson asked if he could drive, so I looked at Sol, who agreed. She then volunteered to sit in the back, and we were on our way.

The I-10 interstate continued on to San Antonio from historic Fort Stockton, but we angled south onto US 285. I would have loved to pay a visit to San Antonio, since I've never been there, but this wasn't the time. Jameson did a great job of driving, so we passed on through the Ciudad Acuña area and had lunch at Eagle Pass, just across the river from Piedras Negras. It ended up being a good call to wait so long for lunch,

The Secret of the Empire

because the border crossing at Laredo proved to be more challenging than I would have preferred.

Jameson eased our SUV up to the Columbia Bridge crossing, because it accesses the divided, multi-lane Monterrey Highway. This is the fastest of the five Ports of Entry, one of which is a railroad crossing. Traffic was moving through quite well, considering other crossings can take an hour or two. When it was our turn, Jameson put the window down and gave a nice greeting. The border agent asked, "Do you have any weapons?" and to my utter shock and disbelief, Jameson said, "Yes." Before the agent could say anything, I nearly yelled, "What are you talking about?" Jameson explained, "You have a pocketknife to cut salami and cheese during our trip."

I put my head down and shook it back and forth as the agent asked, "And who's in the backseat?" I responded, "That's my wife, Sol." That seemed to be sufficient to detain us. He asked Jameson to pull the car over to a parking spot ahead on the left, then told us to get out of the car and sit on the bench. It was all very disturbing, as another agent approached and told us to get out our passports and driver's licenses. He then opened the back of our car and pulled out all three suitcases, leaving the three carry ons in place. As he started going through our luggage, another agent came up to us and asked for our passports. When he walked over to a building with them in hand, that sinking feeling in the pit of my stomach started. I couldn't help but think that if the person in the backseat was another white male, this wouldn't be happening.

We nervously sat there for about twenty minutes, feeling rather violated, particularly because there was nothing we could do. Sol suggested it was a bad idea for her to come, and I quickly put that thought to rest. The agent rummaging through

The Secret of the Empire

our belongings put them back in the trunk and closed it. Soon after that, the agent with our passports returned them and said, "You're good to go."

We got back in the car, and Jameson announced that he didn't feel much like driving. I took over, and we finally continued our journey. Sol hoped this wasn't a harbinger of things to come, so she said, "My culture certainly has its share of superstitions. I'm praying things start going better." Meanwhile, Jameson settled into the back seat and wrapped his mind around being busy on his phone. The final leg of this trip was a little over three hours, and it went uneventfully. We pulled into town just before dark and checked into Quinta Real Monterrey.

All three of us were amazed at the beauty of the hotel, and Jameson quickly retorted, "Hey Mom, you should've seen some of the dumps Geraldo had us stay in last year."

As I laughed, to make sure Sol knew it was a joke, I realized this place really was magnificent, and I couldn't believe the great price. Once we got to our room, we quickly settled in, then went downstairs for dinner. After the meal, I said, "It's been a great day."

"You enjoyed the border crossing?" asked Sol.

"Sorry, you're right. Let's just get a good night's sleep, so we're ready to begin hearing about the prophetic books of the shamans."

ACT I
Before the Exile

SCENE ONE
Isaiah 1-39

It was an absolutely glorious morning in Monterrey. The sun glinted off the Sierra Madre Oriental Mountains, as we were getting ready to begin this new experience. I was pleased to find that despite Monterrey being one of the largest cities in Mexico, it was also considered one of the safest. It seemed like everyone we passed by had a friendly greeting, which added to our feeling of comfort. After checking with the concierge for a good spot to talk, we headed to the downtown Macroplaza. It had plenty of green space, fountains, gardens, benches, and museums, with City Hall on one end and the Governor's Palace on the other. We chose a great spot, with spectacular views of the mountains, and I was hoping Jameson and Sol were excited to get started. I stepped out in front of the two of them sitting on the wood and iron bench, and opened my copy of the Aztec Scriptures.

"Really, Dad?"

I asked him, "What?"

"Geraldo never had to open the scriptures. He just told the stories."

I was a bit flustered because I wasn't sure if Jameson was teasing, so I simply continued. "This is not where Isaiah prophesied." That got their attention. "He was a shaman from the capital city of Tenochtitlan, and he was prophesying to the king of the Southern Empire."

"So why aren't we there?" Jameson asked, but quickly realized that last year's trip brought the context of the Southern Empire alive, so we didn't need to revisit. Then he said, "But I feel bad for Mom, since she wasn't with us."

"Mi hijo," spoke up Sol. "What you don't know is that I was there several times through my childhood, and I am very well acquainted with what it is like."

Jameson looked surprised and asked, "Did you see the ruins of Templo Mayor in the middle of Mexico City?"

"Of course, now let's listen to your father."

"The first thing to understand about the prophecies of Isaiah is that the scriptures we have today are edited. Actually, the book of Isaiah is a combination of three different shamans over two hundred years of time. The first thirty-nine chapters are called First Isaiah, and they take place before the exile. Chapters 40-55 share stories from the exile, and 56-66 take place after the exile. That is critically important to properly understand the prophecies of the shamans. Also, these prophecies can be referred to as oracles.

"So, imagine Isaiah standing before the king in front of the Templo Mayor, when he delivers this word from God. Since Isaiah was a local shaman, the king knew him and was ready to listen. Isaiah took something from his pocket and chewed on it, then went into a trance and shared the vision that came to him. It was not one the king wanted to hear, because it was about God taking the Southern Empire to court. Here's how the oracle went:

'The LORD said, I reared children and brought them up, but they have rebelled against me. Mexico does not know me. My people do not understand me. They are a sinful nation, laden with iniquity. They despise me! Remove the evil of your doings from before my eyes. Cease to do evil, learn to do good, seek justice, rescue the oppressed, defend the orphan, and plead for the widow. If you refuse and rebel, you shall be devoured by the sword; for the mouth of the LORD has spoken.'

"The shaman continued in a rather unexpected way. The vision became a lament for a while, then he offered a promise of restoration: 'Therefore says the Sovereign, the LORD of hosts, the Mighty One; I will pour out my wrath on my enemies. I will turn my hand against you. Then I will purify you with fire. And I will restore your judges as at the first, and your counselors as at the beginning. Afterward you shall be called the city of righteousness, the faithful city.'"

"Wow!" exclaimed Jameson. "I wonder how the king and his people took that."

"We'll never know for sure," I said. "It was great being at Templo Mayor, to get the context of the environment, but we don't know how the people responded. We can guess, and that's part of what Bible Study is all about. So, what's your guess?"

Jameson was the first to respond, saying, "It was a good news, bad news oracle. I guess the people responded out of their own context. If they were having problems, they probably heard the bad news, while those not having difficulties probably paid more attention to the good news."

"I'm impressed, Jameson," added Sol, "but I personally suspect that the Mexican culture would tend to notice the bad news. That's just me speaking, as a Mexican living in America, so take it for what it's worth."

Jameson laughed and said, "Ah, yes. And I notice your 'suspecting' is suspiciously like suspicion. I suppose you can take the Mexican out of Mexico, but you can't take Mexico out of the Mexican."

"Of course," said Sol, "I was born in the United States, making me Mexican-American, but I appreciate the sentiment."

The Secret of the Empire

I said, "We don't know how much later it was before Isaiah offered his next oracle, but it was a vision of the near future. That makes me think they might have been more intrigued with the good news. Anyway, there's a verse in the second chapter of Isaiah that became so famous, it was included on a sculpture that was given to the United Nations by the USSR on December 4th, 1959:

> 'they shall beat their swords into plowshares,
> and their spears into pruning hooks;
> nation shall not lift up sword against nation,
> neither shall they learn war any more.'

"So that's where that came from!" exclaimed Jameson, with a raised eyebrow and a grin of learning something new.

"The rest of the chapter was about judgment against arrogance. This oracle was undoubtedly received well because it was against the Northern Empire."

Even Sol laughed at that one, then said, "You might speak lower, since we are currently in what was the Northern Empire."

Looking around with that realization, I soon calmed myself and said, "Not to worry. The next chapter returns to judgment against the Southern Empire. That oracle personifies the capital city of Tenochtitlan as a woman. Here's an example: 'Instead of perfume there will be a stench; and instead of a sash, a rope; and instead of lovely hair, baldness; and instead of a rich robe, a binding of sackcloth; instead of beauty, shame.'"

"That sounds horrible," complained Sol. "What does it mean?"

"It was a cultural nod back then to women and their role in mourning, while using them as a metaphor for condemnation.

The Secret of the Empire

Then there's a series of oracles denouncing social injustice. The first lament is over those who amass wealth at the expense of others. The second one is about drunkenness and the third is about persistent sinners and skeptics. The fourth is about fake news." Jameson complained that I was going too fast, then requested a sample. I opened my Bible and read Isaiah 5:20: 'Ah, you who call evil good and good evil, who put darkness for light and light for darkness, who put bitter for sweet and sweet for bitter!'"

After quick nods from both Jameson and Sol, I continued. "Just two more laments. The fifth is about self-righteousness: 'Ah, you who are wise in your own eyes, and shrewd in your own sight!'

"I had a professor like that this past year," said Jameson with a frown.

"The sixth is about drunkenness and the perversion of justice: 'Ah, you who are heroes in drinking wine and valiant at mixing drink, who acquit the guilty for a bribe, and deprive the innocent of their rights!'"

"I ran into a few college students like that, too," said Jameson.

"Stay away from them," counseled Sol, and I mentioned that you can find those types anywhere.

"Interestingly, the next chapter is a flashback to Isaiah's call to be a prophetic shaman. He saw the LORD in the Templo Mayor and said, 'Woe is me! I am lost, for I am a man of unclean lips; yet I have seen the LORD of hosts! Then a supernatural being touched my mouth with a burning coal and said, "Your guilt has departed and your sin is blotted out." Then I heard the voice of the Lord saying, "Whom shall I send?" And I said, here am I; send me!'"

The Secret of the Empire

"So that's where the song comes from," smiled Jameson.

"The next chapter has a great illustration of the challenge of hearing prophecies today. Let me just read it. 'Therefore the Lord himself will give you a sign. Look, the young woman is with child and shall bear a son, and shall name him Manuel.'"

"Hey, that's familiar!" testified Jameson. "Our pastor always read it at Christmas because it's a prophecy about the advent of Jim Caldwell, who was God with us."

"Okay, let's look at that. First of all, prophecies were always offered about the near future. If the vision is about war, it would be difficult to get the people concerned about something that was hundreds of years away."

"Okay. So far I'm following you," said Jameson, but Sol folded her arms as if to say she was closed to my thoughts.

"This prophecy is about war, and remember what I said about the importance of context. The king of the Southern Empire experienced an attempted attack on Tenochtitlan by the king of the Northern Empire and the king of Guatemala. Even though it was thwarted, it left the king and his empire in fear. That's when the LORD sent Isaiah to say to the southern king, 'Do not fear, and do not let your heart be troubled. If you do not stand firm in faith, you shall not stand at all.'

"Then the LORD spoke to the southern king, saying 'Ask a sign of the LORD your God.' But the king said, 'I will not ask, and I will not put the LORD to the test.' Then Isaiah said, 'Is it too little for you to weary mortals, that you weary my God also? Therefore the Lord himself will give you a sign. Look, the young woman is with child and shall bear a son, and shall name him Manuel.'

"Whoa!" said Jameson. "Is that true?"

"It's scripture, and our task is to understand it."

The Secret of the Empire

"So this isn't about Jim Caldwell?" asked Jameson. Sol was beginning to squirm on the bench, but I pressed on.

"That's the great thing. Once we understand the prophecy for who it was spoken to, and what it meant at the time, we can then say, 'Hey! I can also learn something about Jim Caldwell.' The point is, we must not ignore its original meaning. Here's the most important thing I'm going to say on this whole trip."

> The Caldwellian Scriptures
> (known as the New Testament)
> can learn from the Aztec Scriptures
> (known as the Old Testament),
> but
> the Old Testament
> can't learn from the New Testament.

"Break time," requested Jameson. "I'm going to need to think about that one for a while."

We agreed, and headed off for a little stroll. The Macroplaza, or La Gran Plaza, is the fifth largest plaza in the world. We soon came to a spectacular fountain and decided to settle in there to hear more.

"Honestly, Dad. I'm struggling with the last idea."

"Let me put it this way. The present can learn from the past, but the past can't learn from the present."

"I think that's better, but I'm still going to need more time to think."

"Try this. When it comes to the first part, about the present learning from the past, Winston Churchill said it best. 'Those who fail to learn from history are doomed to repeat it.'

"So why is it bad to see Isaiah's prophecy being about Jim

The Secret of the Empire

Caldwell?"

"It isn't. As long as we first acknowledge that we have learned what it meant in its historical setting, and then learn how we might use it for fresh understandings in the New Testament."

"Then what about the second part, that the past can't learn from the present?"

"That's akin to fortune telling. The prophets were simply sharing about the near future. That a young woman would soon bear a child, who would signify God's presence, which was meant to convince the king that God was with the Southern Kingdom and Tenochtitlan. There was no implication about a future child named Jim Caldwell."

"But then we can say, 'Wow, Jim Caldwell was like that too, because he signifies God's presence in our life. Right?" asked Jameson.

"I think you've got it. What do you think, Sol?"

"I'm where Jameson was earlier, when he said he needed to think about it for a while."

"Fair enough. Are we ready to continue?" They nodded their heads, and I started into another misunderstood prophecy, hoping I had set the stage properly. "I'm sure this one is familiar, from the second verse of Isaiah 9:

> The people who walked in darkness
>   have seen a great light;
> those who lived in a land of deep darkness—
>   on them light has shined.

"So, that's not about Jim Caldwell either?" asked Jameson with a bit of intrigue, mixed with a minor sense of loss.

"The Caldwellian tradition sees it as a description of the

The Secret of the Empire

coming Messiah, but actually it is a celebration of the coronation of a new king of the Southern Empire. It was particularly hopeful because the Northern Empire had already been overthrown, and the people needed a good word. Isaiah comes along and offers the positive idea that this new king would have a glorious reign, and the two empires would reunite."

"So, if it's okay to learn from the Old Testament, how was Jim Caldwell similar to that verse?" inquired my properly inquisitive son.

"Great question! In my opinion, the Wild West that Jim Caldwell came to in 1881 was full of darkness. It had constant Indian raids, rampant gambling, alcoholism, prostitution, and of course, the Russian Invasion. The good news that Jim Caldwell brought was that we could love one another in spite of the challenges all around. His stories and miracles became a light that shined in the darkness."

Sol spoke up at that point, saying, "I'm still thinking about all of this, but most importantly I am beginning to see that this new way of understanding prophecy could enhance my belief."

I've got to admit, I was glad to hear that. Sol had been so kind to let us go to Mexico last year, and it is great having her with us now, so I relaxed a bit as I continued. "Just a few verses later, in verse six, we get another example of how Caldwellians have misappropriated an ancient text:

For a child has been born for us,
a son given to us;
authority rests upon his shoulders;
and he is named
Wonderful Counselor, Mighty God,
Everlasting Father, Prince of Peace.

The Secret of the Empire

"Don't take that away from me!" announced Sol with furrowed eyebrows. "Jim was born for us, was given to us, has authority, and lived like those titles. And that ends it."

Maybe it was time for me to soften things. Sol was raised in the Catholic faith, then became an evangelistic Caldwellian, and knows her Bible. "I'm not trying to take anything from you. It is fine to hold on to your understandings. The purpose of this trip is to see the places where the shamans delivered their oracles and appreciate what they meant then. Let me repeat. We can learn from the Old Testament. It is fine to say that Jim Caldwell was just like that ancient oracle."

"Don't sugar coat it, Dad. Remind us what it is that's not fine to do."

Sol remained quite emphatic that she wanted this prophecy to be about Jim, so I proceeded, well, how shall we say it? Lovingly. "The past doesn't know the future any more than we do." I looked at my wife and said, "Honey, just let the Holy Bible say what it means."

"Still going to need some time," Sol said earnestly.

"That's fine."

"So," asked Jameson, "what does Isaiah 9:6 mean?"

"Back then the people believed that the king was reborn as God's son at the time of his coronation. Wonderful Counselor, and the other names, were titles given to the king of Guatemala at his coronation, so Isaiah appropriated those titles. This verse is an ecstatic celebration of hope in difficult times. Isaiah went on to describe the destruction of the Northern Kingdom, as a warning that the Southern Kingdom needed to change its ways." Jameson looked happy, but Sol didn't. I had to accept that not everyone likes serious bible study. Taking scripture at surface level is much easer.

The Secret of the Empire

"Isaiah went on with an oracle against Colombia. Here's an example: 'When the Lord has finished all his work on Tenochtitlan, he will punish the arrogant boasting of the king of Colombia and his haughty pride.' He then shares a promise that a remnant of the people of the Northern Kingdom will be saved. After that, he shares an oracle about what the ideal king would be like:

> A shoot shall come out from the stump of King
>   Montezuma, and a branch shall grow out of his roots.
> The spirit of the LORD shall rest on him,
>   the spirit of wisdom and understanding,
>   the spirit of counsel and might,
>   the spirit of knowledge, and the fear of the LORD,
>   which shall be his delight.

"See!" Sol said with a smile. "Jim's ancestor was King Montezuma."

"Yes!" I said with a similar smile. "We can learn from the Old Testament. That's great. So what do you think Isaiah was meaning for the people of his time?"

"You already told us, Dad. He painted a picture of what a great king would be like."

"Thanks, Jameson. I think the ideal king was Montezuma's son. Then, in 11:6, Isaiah paints a picture of what peace and harmony would like, once an ideal king was crowned:

> The wolf shall live with the lamb,
>   the coyote shall lie down with pups,
> the calf and the mountain lion will be together,
>   and a little child will lead them.

The Secret of the Empire

"Yes", said Sol, "and the little child became Jim Caldwell."

"And just maybe," I said softly, "this oracle could be about hope in a king at that particular time. Of course we see the ideal way things could have worked out for Jim, but they didn't. The sheriff and Russian overlord won with their evil."

"And Jim taught us to be peacemakers," responded Sol.

"Okay," I suggested, "maybe we're ready for lunch."

Jameson immediately spoke up and said, "I was checking on Tripadvisor this morning and found a great spot. Fonda El Limoncito. Travelers say the food is delicious, the place is comfortable, the service is impeccable, and Chef Juan Pablo even comes out to greet his customers."

"Okay," announced Sol, "but how far away?"

"That's the best thing! It's only about three blocks away," said Jameson with a huge smile.

We set off for a pleasant walk, but it turned out to be more than three blocks, because we were quite a bit north in the Macroplaza. First we passed the Faro de Comercio monument, then angled through several busy city streets before getting there. It was in a century-old house, with bare stone walls and a tall ceiling, in the heart of the Old Town. To say the least, we had a great experience, and sure enough the happy Chef passed by with a friendly welcome. On the way out, I was anxious to hear what Sol thought, and was delightfully surprised when she said it was reminiscent of her mother's home cooking.

The weather was a stunning 77 degrees, and no wind. For the afternoon we settled in across the street from the Archdiocese of Monterrey Catholic Church, mainly because there was a public restroom nearby. After the c-section birth of Jameson, Sol had a prolapsed bladder and needed bathroom breaks more often. I stepped out in front of them, and began.

The Secret of the Empire

"The next eleven chapters of Isaiah consists of oracles against the countries that fought wars with Mexico, but I want to deal with chapter 14. It has another one of those highly misunderstood verses. Its verse 12, and here it is: "How you are fallen from heaven, O Day Star, son of Dawn!""

Sol had a rather visceral reaction to this verse. Her arms quickly went back to a folded position, and her whole body screamed of a lack of interest. She finally spoke up, saying, "Why would you want to talk about the devil?" Talk about thin ice. I'd never really shared any of my biblical understandings with Sol before, but I guessed her Catholic background was speaking louder than me.

Jameson was understandably intrigued, so I proceeded carefully. Admittedly, I felt about as clumsy as a bull trying to make its way through a china shop. "When the Caldwellian Scriptures were translated into Spanish, this verse used the word '*angel caido*,' for 'fallen from heaven,' meaning fallen angel. What's worse is when 'Day Star' was translated into Spanish it became '*lucifero*,' meaning light-bearer. Soon after that, Caldwellian fantasy ran wild about a 'Lucifer' falling from heaven."

"That's because we know our Holy Scriptures," scowled Sol. She then grabbed my Bible and turned to Revelation 12:7-9 and read, 'And war broke out in heaven; Michael and his angels fought against the dragon. The dragon and his angels fought back, but they were defeated, and there was no longer any place for them in heaven. The great dragon was thrown down, that ancient serpent, who is called the Devil and Satan, the deceiver of the whole world—he was thrown down to the earth, and his angels were thrown down with him.'" She then slapped the book back into my hands in a triumphant gesture.

The Secret of the Empire

"Okay, yet again, let me say that I'm not trying to change your understandings of the Bible. I'm just giving you possibilities to consider." I then cupped my hand to target my voice to Jameson and whispered, "Not very considerate if you ask me." Without hesitation she responded, "I heard that!" I wasn't sure how to proceed at that point, because I love studying the book of Revelation, but the focus of the trip was to hear the prophets in their context.

"Let me take a moment to say what I think Isaiah 14:12 was about. No matter how much one might want that verse to be about Lucifer falling from heaven, it simply wasn't, for two reasons. First, remember that the Old Testament can't learn from the New Testament. Second, let Isaiah speak for himself, because he tells us who this verse is about. Verse 4 says 'You will take up this taunt against the king of Spain.' See. It's not about Lucifer at all. God gave this oracle to Isaiah about the downfall of the King of Spain. The place where God's children were treated so poorly, before they escaped and began their journey to the Promised Land. Verse 12 was almost like a laughter about how far the King had fallen from his heavenly heights of power."

"Wow!" exclaimed Jameson. "I love that."

Sol wasn't affected quite the same way, but I went on. "The oracles from Isaiah came in fast and furious after that. He pronounced prophecies against Belize, Honduras, El Salvador, Nicaragua, Costa Rica, Panama, and Colombia, ending with a warning of destruction of Tenochtitlan. That last oracle was spoken to the people of the Southern Empire. The caution was about being sure the people didn't get too happy, because their exultation could be premature. That twenty-second chapter ends with a denunciation of ego: 'On that day, says the LORD of hosts, the peg that was fastened in a secure place will give way; it will be cut down and fall, and the load that was on it will perish, for the LORD has spoken.'

"Chapters 24-27 contain what is known as 'The Isaiah Apocalypse.' The material is very different, because it is not a prophetic speech. The lengthy oracles against nations that just concluded, give way to announcements about the whole earth and all who live in it. It is a proclamation of the final drama of history, dealing with the last things. People who study the Bible are beginning to see that it isn't an apocalypse in the truest sense. It doesn't give a detailed revelation of the future. In my opinion, the difference between prophecy and apocalypse is that prophecy is about the near future, and apocalypse is about the distant future. They are similar in that they both concern revelation from God."

"How do you know so much?" asked Jameson.

"I love the Bible and I love to study. That said, please remember that I'm no expert. These are thoughts from scholars, put in the best way I know how." I then opened my copy of the Bible and said, "Here's some thoughts that Isaiah shared:

- See, the LORD is going to lay waste the earth and devastate it; he will ruin its face and scatter its inhabitants...The earth will be completely laid waste and totally plundered. The LORD has spoken this word.—Isaiah 24:1, 3.
- On this mountain he will destroy the shroud that enfolds all peoples, the sheet that covers all nations; he will swallow up death forever. The Sovereign LORD will wipe away the tears from all faces; he will remove the disgrace of his people from all the earth.

The LORD has spoken.—Isaiah 25:7-8.

- Open the gates that the righteous nation may enter, the nation that keeps faith.—Isaiah 26:2.
- In days to come the Southern Empire shall take root, the Northern Empire shall blossom and put forth shoots, and fill the whole world with fruit.—Isaiah 27:6.

"It does seem a bit disjointed," Jameson observed.

"I liked it," added Sol.

I announced that I was ready to move on to chapters 28-33, and having no objections, I started. "This is really the final section of First Isaiah. It leads up to the time of the fall of the Southern Empire to Cortés and the Spanish Conquistadors, but begins with an oracle about the fall of the Northern Empire. Verse 7 basically says that the South needs to learn from the North. Isaiah castigates the priests and prophets who 'reel with strong drink,' and scolds them with, 'they err in vision, they stumble in giving judgment.'

"Isaiah goes on in the 16th verse to give hope to the Southern Empire: 'therefore thus says the Lord GOD, See I am laying in Tenochtitlan a foundation stone, a tested stone, a precious cornerstone, a sure foundation: "One who trusts will not panic."' Chapter 29 describes the siege of Tenochtitlan. He says that God will encamp against them, just as King Montezuma originally did to capture the city."

"Okay," said a frustrated Jameson, "I'm lost. Is this oracle about hope or despair?"

I said, "Yes. The despair is about the overthrow of Tenochtitlan, and the hope is about its ultimate salvation."

Sol spoke up at that point and said, "Sounds like Good

The Secret of the Empire

Friday and Easter."

"Thanks," I said. "I kind of like that. It even fits with verse 18, 'On that day the deaf shall hear the words of a scroll, and out of their gloom and darkness the eyes of the blind shall see.'"

Sol then said, "Sounds like the Old Testament was learning from the New Testament." Her arms were again folded and a mild scowl crept across her face.

"I know what you mean, honey, and you may be teaching me something here. Let's go on."

"Okay," said Jameson, "but I hope this gets less tedious."

At first I was offended, then I decided to try to learn something from my son. "In what way is it tedious?"

"Probably because Geraldo just told the stories."

"Good point. The difference might be that the first part of the Aztec Scriptures is simply stories. So now I'm trying to think about why the prophetic stories aren't the same." I paused for a while and saw blank stares from Jameson and Sol. "Maybe it's because I'm explaining them, while Geraldo told them." Jameson then suggested that I quit explaining them, and just let the stories speak for themselves. It took me a while to respond to that one, but I finally spoke up and said, "I'll try, but to be honest, explanation is sometimes needed to keep the story from being misunderstood. The good thing is that the other prophets aren't as long as Isaiah."

"I agree," said Jameson, and Sol almost simultaneously said, "that's a very good thing." Jameson and Sol smiled at each other and winked.

"Then let me wrap up this first part of Isaiah as fast as I can. As the story goes," I said with a mild smirk of my own, "Isaiah warned the Southern Empire not to work with Guatemala to fight off Colombia."

"Why?" inquired Jameson.

"Because it would be the LORD who would deliver Tenochtitlan from a Colombian attack. After that, a king would arise and reign in righteousness. The prophecy then closes with an oracle against Colombia."

"Wait," announced Jameson. "What chapter is that?"

"Good catch. It's only chapter 33. Chapters 34-39 have long been debated by biblical scholars, and many believe they are sufficiently different from First Isaiah."

"In what way?" asked Sol. I was surprised but pleased with her question.

"It's in both style and substance."

"How can that be?" she continued.

"Okay. Here's a big picture of the Aztec Scriptures. It all started with the stories of Aapo and Abund being told from generation to generation. After Geovanni led God's people out of Guatemala and into the Promised Land of Mexico, the verbal Aztec language learned writing. The stories were written down and edited, to get to the Old Testament we know today. My point is that Chapters 34-39 appear to be later edited additions, so I'm just going skip to them." I was mildly surprised when they had no problems with my plan, so I happily went on.

"We've completed the first of fifteen prophets, and I'm pleased about how it's gone." I then looked at Jameson and asked, "Remember when Geraldo would from time to time ask what we've learned?" Jameson nodded, so I said, "Let's try that. What have you learned so far, even though we're standing in the place of the capital of the Northern Empire, while mostly hearing stories about the capital of the Southern Empire?"

Sol was quick to respond. "I was impressed how brave Isaiah must have been to offer a gloom and doom prophecy to the king. I guess I was thinking of medieval times, when the court jester could lose his head if he didn't humor the king."

Jameson immediately spoke up and said, "I had no idea the book of Isaiah contained prophecies of three different people from three different times."

"I liked," Sol offered, "that the young woman bore a son and named him Manuel, which means God with us. It is wonderful to have my understandings of the Bible confirmed because Jim Caldwell became God with us."

A little smoke must have been noticeably rising from the top of my head, so Jameson tried to lighten up the situation. "I loved it that Isaiah induced his visions by chewing on something. Maybe peyote buttons?"

I said, "Probably."

Jameson then Googled it and said, "Hey, cool. It says here that Mexican peyote has been used from earliest recorded time by indigenous peoples in northern Mexico and the southwestern part of the United States."

Sol was next. "I liked confirming that the Old Testament can learn from the New Testament."

"Jeez, Mom. Give it a break." I glared at Sol, when I probably should have been upset with my son.

"Maybe Jameson has something worthwhile to say," I suggested.

"Okay. I'm ready," he said. "I really liked the story of Isaiah's call, since I'm thinking about going into ministry, I loved that he heard the voice of God asking who he could send. Then Isaiah's response was almost life changing for me: 'Here I am; send me!'"

I got a bit choked up and noticed a tear falling down Sol's cheek. "Anything else?"

The Secret of the Empire

Jameson said, "I loved learning that the New Testament can learn from the Old Testament, but…"

Sol interrupted with, "You can have your opinion, mi hijo. Meanwhile, I hated the Lucifer story you told."

My eyes must have widened a bit, then I said, "Let's call it a day. Thanks for your attention. I'm ready for dinner and a good night's sleep."

Jameson asked, "What's on the agenda for tomorrow?

"We'll discuss four more of the shamans who prophesied before the exile."

SCENE TWO
Amos, Hosea, Micah, Zephaniah

The morning brought an unexpected rainstorm, so I went downstairs to talk to the concierge. She said it was a passing storm, and would be fine by late morning, so I told her I would like a conference room for the morning if one was available. She very kindly offered to go check, then came back and said that room 137 could be used. I thanked her for her hospitality and headed back upstairs to share the good news. After breakfast, we made our way to the room and got settled in.

It was a pleasant room with plenty of chairs, but we were first attracted to the window. Not for the view of downtown, but to watch the storm for awhile. The clouds billowed in dark shapes, as the rain came down quite hard. Flashes of light off in the distance told me it was already in the moving on stage. The mild thunder was so muffled that it really was no problem for our morning session, so I pulled up a chair toward the front and decided to relax while talking. Sol and Jameson pulled up chairs and we sat in a circle.

Amos

"We'll begin with the prophecy of the shaman Amos. What makes him unique is that he was from the Southern Empire, yet God called him to offer his prophecies to the Northern Empire."

Jameson seemed a bit disappointed, so I asked what was on his mind. He said, "It's just that yesterday we had to remember the context of the Southern Empire, while we heard the prophecies of Isaiah to the capital city of Tenochtitlan. Finally, here we are for today's prophecy to the Northern Empire, and we're still not outside to soak up the context of the capital city of Monterrey."

"I really appreciate that! Just remember we're going to be here for about a week, so we'll have plenty of time to enjoy the city. Besides, there are no ruins here. Nothing historical to see, or at least with respect to the ancient northern capital."

"Why is that?" asked Sol.

"Nobody knows for sure, but it probably has something to do with the secret of the empire."

"Which is?" inquired Jameson.

"No, no, no. Not yet. We're here to enjoy the full experience, so I'll leave that for later. So, back to the shaman. Amos was prophesying while the popular sentiment was that their status as God's people gave them assurance of forgiveness. Amos had an uphill battle because his message was that their special status gave them responsibility, holding them to a higher standard. Amos got started with his drug-induced vision by condemning the nations that went to war against the Mexican Empire."

Jameson interrupted with, "Wait a minute, please. Did Amos share his prophecy to the Northern Empire while he was there, or did he say his words from the safety of his Southern Empire?"

"Great question, as always. Later in his book it becomes evident that he was right here in Monterrey, possibly during a cultic celebration. Amos even used that moment to offer a short prophecy against the Southern Empire for rejecting God's laws."

Sol smiled and said, "I'll bet that was easy for the

The Secret of the Empire

northerners to hear."

"Sure, but Amos quickly turned his judgment back on the north. He first chastises them for ignoring what all God had done for them in the past, including raising up 'some of your children to be prophets.' Then God's punishment is predicted: 'So I will press you down in your place. Flight shall perish from the swift, and the strong shall not retain their strength, nor shall the mighty save their lives...says the LORD' (Amos 2:13-14).

"He continues with this. 'Hear this word that the LORD has spoken against you, O people of the Northern Empire, against the whole family that I brought up out of the land of Guatemala: You only have I known of all the families of the earth; therefore I will punish you for all your iniquities.' Amos then envisions the destruction of the sanctuary at Monterrey: 'Hear, and testify against the Northern Empire, says the LORD. On the day I punish the north for its transgressions, I will punish the altars of Monterrey. I will tear it down and it will come to an end, says the LORD' (Amos 3:13-15).

"Amos goes on in chapter 5 to say 'Fallen, no more to rise, is the Northern Empire; forsaken on her land, with no one to raise her up' (vs. 2). The LORD then offers a way for them to change: 'Seek me and live' (vs. 4). He then offers a warning: 'or he will break out against you like fire, and it will devour Monterrey, with no one to quench it' (vs. 6). After that Amos offers another way out of their problems: 'Seek good and not evil, that you may live' (vs. 14). He then takes direct aim at their problem: 'I hate, I despise your festivals, and I take no delight in your solemn assemblies' (vs. 21)."

"Why are they so despicable?" asked Jameson.

"I know that one!" exclaimed Sol. "Confession without repentance is meaningless."

The Secret of the Empire

"Tell me more, Mom," requested Jameson.

"These were people who confessed their belief in God. That's why they went to the sacred festivals and worshiped, but God didn't like it because they were speaking out of both sides of their mouth. They didn't live a life of repentance. One can't change on the Sabbath, then be evil the rest of the week."

"Got it," announced Jameson. "It reminds me of a lot of people who follow the Caldwellian faith, but one would never know it."

I chimed back in with, "The good news is that Amos didn't just name problems, he offered a solution. Here's probably the best known verse from Amos, in chapter 5, verse 24:

> But let justice roll down like waters,
> and righteousness like an ever-flowing stream.

"How did that work out for Amos?" asked Jameson.

"As you obviously suspect, it got difficult. First of all, Amos had a huge confrontation with the priest of Monterrey, who sent word to the king of the Northern Empire, saying, 'Amos has conspired against you in the very center of Monterrey. He said that you would die by the sword, and the Northern Empire must go into exile away from this land.' A stern response came to Amos from the king: 'O seer, go back where you came from, but never again prophesy at Monterrey, for it is the king's sanctuary, and it is a temple of the kingdom.'

"Then Amos answered the king: 'I am no prophet, I am a herdsman from the Southern Kingdom. But the LORD said to me to prophesy to his people in the Northern Kingdom, so here it is: Your wife shall become a prostitute in the city, and your sons and your daughters shall fall by the sword, and your land shall be parceled out. You yourself shall die in another land, and the Northern Kingdom shall surely go into exile away from this land.'"

"Wow!" exclaimed Jameson. "Talk about gutsy!"

Sol suggested, "I suppose if the LORD gives you a job to do, you ought to do it."

"Well, Amos still wasn't done. In chapter 9 he shares a final vision of the LORD himself standing on the altar in Monterrey and commanding its destruction. Amos then shares imagery depicting no place for the people to hide: not in the depths of Sheol, nor the heights of heaven, nor the tops of mountains, nor the bottom of the sea. He then closes this vision with, 'And though they go into captivity in front of their enemies, there I will command the sword, and it shall kill them; and I will fix my eyes on them for harm and not for good' (vs. 4)."

"Dang!" exclaimed Jameson. "Maybe they should have stayed on God's good side."

We laughed, but it was no laughing matter for the people of the Northern Empire. "While the prophesied exile didn't happen immediately, it happened about twenty years later."

"Can't say they weren't warned," exclaimed Sol.

"Hey, did you hear that?" asked Jameson. I mentioned that I didn't hear anything, and Jameson said, "That's because the storm has passed outside." We all three went to the window and saw the clouds parting and the sun beginning to shine, then Jameson said, "Too bad the people of the Northern Empire couldn't get away from their storm, but then again it was a storm they brought upon themselves."

The telling of the prophet Amos couldn't have gone better, but we were ready to get outside. While Sol and Jameson went to our room to get a few towels to dry off the bench, I headed back to the concierge to get a weather report. I was delighted to hear that it was going to be great for the rest of the day, so when they came back down, we headed for the Macroplaza.

Hosea

Since the green space was so wonderfully large, we looked around for a while, then chose a bench in a new location. We used one towel to dry it off, then put down two others to sit on. As Sol and Jameson settled in, I got ready to talk. Right then the sun cleared from behind a cloud and made an almost eerie spotlight, which didn't go unnoticed by my family. I cleared my throat as I thought about this rather strange prophecy, then prepared to talk.

"The king of the Northern Empire was surely glad when Amos finally went back home, but next up was the shaman Hosea. At least he was a hometown boy, and his vision was ultimately an appeal for the Northern Empire to return to the LORD. The shaman was angry with the alliance the north had with Colombia, because he considered it a rejection of the LORD, and viewed it as idolatry.

"Hosea was a compassionate man who loved his people and was aware of their sin. To symbolize the north's unfaithful relationship with God, the LORD told Hosea to, 'Go, take for yourself a wife of whoredom and have children of whoredom, for the land commits great whoredom by forsaking the LORD.'

"I don't like that," announced Sol.

"It's pretty rough," I agreed, "but here's the point. Amos offered a solution to their problems, while Hosea lived an example of redeeming love. He married the harlot Gomer..."

"Yuck!" Sol just couldn't help from sharing her surprise.

"They then had children and gave them symbolic names."

"Okay," complained Sol, "you just don't do that. Names are everything!"

"This probably won't help, but it was a metaphor for the bad relationship the people of the north had with God."

"Correct, as usual," Sol said curtly, "but not helpful."

"I think it's time to check out Hosea's speeches against the north. They were designed to get the Northern Empire to repent of their ways. Hosea basically asks his people to learn from him, with this: 'She shall pursue her lovers, but not overtake them, and she shall seek them, but shall not find them. Then she shall say, "I will go and return to my first husband, for it was better with me then than now" (Hosea 2:7).

"I get it!" said Jameson. "Hosea wants his people to see that they are like harlots who have run off with other men, but they would be better off by being faithful to the LORD." I smiled, and Sol folded her arms.

"Verse 13 get less symbolic and more direct. 'I will punish her for the festival days of the gods, when she offered incense to them and decked herself with her ring and jewelry, and went after her lovers, and forgot me, says the LORD.' After that, the speech moves on to Hosea trying to win his wife back. Unfortunately, Sol, chapter 3 turns bad again." I could barely bring myself to look at her, but the story must go on. "The LORD told Hosea to love an adulterous woman."

"That's it!" exclaimed Sol. "You just keep right on talking while I take a restroom break. Maybe by the time I get back, the story will be better, or maybe even finished."

As she left, I was a bit uncomfortable because we were out of the country. The restroom was within eyesight, but I just didn't feel like continuing. Jameson understood, so we started chatting about last year's tour. The great memories just came flooding back, and I was so happy that event happened. I was also hopeful that this event would prove useful.

"Here she comes," whispered Jameson in an almost scared tone.

I looked at him, shook my head and said, "No, we have to be honest with her."

As she settled back onto the bench next to Jameson, she said, "I hope you've made good progress."

When I assured her we had, Jameson shot me a look that made it obvious I failed the test of honesty. "Anyway, Hosea shared the thought that the Northerners would indeed return and seek the LORD. In chapter 4 he shares the word of the LORD; 'for the LORD has an indictment against the inhabitants of the land. There is no faithfulness or loyalty, and no knowledge of God in the land' (vs. 1). He then points the finger at the priesthood for failing to hold the people accountable to the covenant.

"Next, Hosea moves into lengthy oracles against the north. In 5:6 he says, 'With their flocks and herds they shall go to seek the LORD, but they will not find him; he has withdrawn from them.' Hosea gives an extended speech from God, mainly explaining that their punishment is due to the alliance the Northern Empire made with Guatemala and Colombia. In chapter 6 he says, 'Come, let us return to the LORD; for it is he who has torn, and he will heal us; he has struck down, and he will bind us up. After two days he will revive us; on the third day he will raise us up, that we may live before him' (vss. 1-2).

"Wonderful!" celebrated Sol. "Jim Caldwell was raised on the third day, so it sounds like the Old Testament is once again learning form the New Testament."

"That's fine," I said. "We all understand scripture in whatever way speaks best to us." It was obvious Sol was done thinking about it, so I went on. "Next the oracle complains about impenitence. Isaiah reports that God says to the Northern Empire, 'Your love is like a morning cloud, like the dew that goes away early.' (6:4). In the following chapter he says, 'the Northern Empire's pride humbles them; yet they do not return to the LORD their God, or seek him' (7:10). God even says, 'Woe to them, for they have strayed from me! Destruction to them, for they have rebelled against me! I would redeem them, but they speak lies against me' (7:13). God then levels his charge against both empires: 'The north has forgotten his Maker, and built palaces; and the south has multiplied fortified cities; but I will send a fire upon his cities, and it shall devour his strongholds' (8:14).

Jameson broke into the story and said, "Is that God speaking or Hosea?"

"Yes. The words alternate between the messenger and the message so much, that sometimes it's difficult telling the difference. This verse seems to be an interesting combination: 'The days of punishment have come, the days of recompense have come; the Northern Empire cries, "The prophet is a fool, the man of the spirit is mad!" Because of your great iniquity, your hostility is great' (9:7).

"So," continued Jameson, "Hosea was complaining about how he was being treated, while his task was to let the people know that the LORD was being mistreated."

"Yes! Very good. It's hard to not take things personally, even if you have a divine task. Here's Hosea's next response: 'Because they have not listened to him, my God will reject them;

they shall become wanderers among the nations' (9:17).

Sol said that she heard one of her Caldwellian Church pastors talk about this verse. "He used the image of 'the wandering Aztec' to justify persecution of today's Mexicans when they don't accept Jim Caldwell."

Jameson asked her, "How does that make you feel as a Mexican, Mom?"

She responded with, "It seems to me to be stereotyping, and prejudice, and discrimination, and hatred, all rolled into one." Her body told the same story as she folded her arms and crossed her legs.

I said, "It sounds like we have to be careful with the way we interpret scripture."

She shocked me when she replied, "Maybe sometimes we shouldn't try to make the Old Testament learn from the New Testament." Jameson's jaw dropped and he gave her a spontaneous hug.

When we were ready to proceed, I said, "All I know is that I love the Bible. Its difficult trying to understand what it says, and even tougher to interpret what it means. But spending time with it is time well spent." They both nodded, then I went on. "Check this out. 'When the Empire was a child, I loved him, and out of Guatemala I called my son' (11:1)."

Sol said, "Okay, now that one's about Jim!"

Jameson and I just looked at each other, then I said, "Sure, hon, if that's what you need, just stick with it. I just love it when Hosea's prejudice creeps in, like in 11:12, he seems to offer God's complaint that the North is lying and deceitful about God, but the South 'still walks with God, and is faithful to the Holy One.' Chapter 13 recalls the exodus and the wilderness wanderings to show God's original good intentions toward the

The Secret of the Empire

North, while chapter 14 is a plea for repentance.

"The book concludes with an assurance of forgiveness, if they reject their idolatrous ways. The final verse is a call to understand God's righteousness: 'Those who are wise understand these things; those who are discerning know them. For the ways of the LORD are right, and the upright walk in them, but transgressors stumble in them' (vs. 9). Okay. That's gotten us through the first two prophets. Let's go to lunch, then this afternoon we'll tackle Micah and Zephaniah."

Micah

The afternoon turned into a gorgeous day, as the sun shone bright and glistened off the tall downtown buildings. Even though the temperature was in the high eighties, the mild breeze made it feel cooler and the humidity was thankfully low. Being from Arizona, my family struggles with any muggy environment. We settled into yet another location in the Macroplaza and prepared for the next shamanic vision.

"Micah prophesied the fall of Tenochtitlan, and the destruction of Templo Mayor. What made him unique was that he was a commoner from the south, speaking to the people of the capital city, and he was prophesying at the edge of the north's demise. Here's how it starts: "The word of the LORD that came to Micah of San Miguel Ajusco in the days of three kings of the Southern Empire."

"Ah, yes. I remember it well," exclaimed Sol. We looked at her with confused expressions, so she said, "Another reference to Jim." When that didn't bring clarity, she said, "Don't you remember the three kings from the birth story of Jim?" I muddled out the words, "maybe we find what we're looking for," but that went about as well as running over a skunk.

"Maybe we should just continue," I offered. To be honest, I was surprised that Sol and I had never discussed these things. Our faith is very important to us, but I think our upbringing had an even bigger impact on our theology. "Micah's vision called for the people to hear and listen. I kind of like that. Its one thing to hear someone, and a totally different experience when one listens. Anyway, his vision was not easy to hear, so they really needed to listen. The LORD said through his prophet, 'I will make Tenochtitlan a heap in the open country' (vs. 6). Micah then shared that he would mourn for them, and that they should mourn for themselves.

"He goes on to denounce their wickedness, saying, 'They covet fields, and seize them; houses, and take them away' (2:2). The people don't like what they are hearing, so they disagree: 'one should not preach of such things; disgrace will not overtake us' (2:6). Next the prophet turns his attention to the leaders: 'Hear this, you rulers who abhor justice and pervert all equity' (3:9), 'because of you the Temple shall be plowed as a field; Tenochtitlan shall become a heap of ruins, and the mountain of the house a wooded height' (3:12).

"At that point the vision turns to hope. 'In days to come the mountain of the LORD's house shall be established as the highest of the mountains, and shall be raised up above the hills. Peoples shall stream to it, and many nations shall come and say: "Come, let us go up to the mountain of the LORD, to the house of the God of Mexica; that he may teach us his ways and that we may walk in his paths"' (4:1-2). Those days would come, but the sinful people are still going to have to endure exile: 'for now you shall go forth from the city and camp in the open country; you shall be conquered by the Spanish, but you shall be rescued' (4:10).

"Here the vision turns again, talking about the siege of Tenochtitlan. 'Now you are walled around with a wall, siege is laid against us; with a rod they strike the ruler of the Southern Empire upon the cheek.' (5:1)."

"Wait a minute," requested Jameson. "Did Micah just include himself as part of the ones who will be sieged?"

"Yes. Remember that he was from there. He was one of them. He just had a task to do as called upon by God. I don't really want to read the next verse, but I will. 'But you, O Texcoco de Mora, who are one of the little clans of the Southern Empire, from you shall come forth for me one who is to rule in Mexico, whose origin is from of old, from ancient days' (5:2)."

"Thanks," said a grinning Sol. "We all know that's about Jim Caldwell. Case closed."

First I caught myself folding my arms, but quickly unfolded them. Knowing that rebuttal would be futile, I continued on. "Chapter 6 shifts back to the present day, with God taking the people to a metaphorical court: 'O my people, what have I done to you? In what have I wearied you? Answer me!' (vs. 3). There is no answer, because they were wrong. They just needed a solution to their problem, and they got a good one.

'He has told you, O mortal, what is good;
and what does the LORD require of you
but to do justice, and to love kindness,
and to walk wisely with your God' (vs.8).

"I have a question," mentioned Jameson with a quizzical look.

"Of course, go ahead."

"This great verse is something even some of the college kids talk about, but it never hit me until now. Since this was a prophecy of gloom and doom, I think it would be much tougher to practice if you're being told a disaster was looming."

"My son!" exclaimed Sol. "That's a great point. Its one thing to live a proper life, but I think God is very interested in how we react in the midst of problems."

Great comments from my wife and son caused us to pause for a bit. The beautiful weather, friendly people, and lovely views were certainly a blessing, so we chatted for a while about living Micah 6:8 when life wasn't so good. Sol offered a dramatic example. "When I was in high school, my class visited Cartolandia, on the southwest side of Mexico City."

"What's that?" asked Jameson.

"Literally a city of houses made from cardboard boxes, usually with a tin roof over it. It was the poorest of the poor who lived there, but it wasn't heartbreaking. The people were full of joy and hope. We visited on a Saturday, and several people invited us to come to church the next morning. After the teacher figured out how to adjust his agenda, we went. That church was filled with more praise than any place I've ever been."

"Wow! Thanks Mom, that's inspiring."

Finding good in challenging times was a truth to savor. I wanted to bask in this moment, but my agenda-driven personality forced me to move on. The final chapter shares the prophet's anger: 'The faithful have disappeared from the land, and there is no one left who is upright' (7:2). He then shares his personal response: 'But as for me, I will look to the LORD, I will wait for the God of my salvation; my God will hear me' (7:7).

"Micah closes with making sure that listeners understand

The Secret of the Empire

God as the compassionate one:

> 'Who is a God like you, pardoning iniquity
> > and passing over the transgression
> of the remnant of your possession?
> > He does not retain his anger forever,
> because he delights in showing clemency.
> > He will again have compassion on us;
> he will tread our iniquities under foot.
> > You will cast all our sins
> into the depths of the sea.
> > You will show faithfulness to Mexica
> and unswerving loyalty to Aapo,
> > as you have sworn to our ancestors
> from the days of old' (7:18-20)."

The Fall of the North to the Colombians

"Remember when I talked about a time when the Colombians lost a war against Mexico?"

"No," answered Sol.

A bit puzzled, I thought maybe my wife wasn't listening very well. Then Jameson said, "That was from last year's trip, Dad."

Relieved, I said, "A quick refresher. Not all of the Colombians returned to Colombia. Some took their boats north and settled in the state of Sinaloa. There they became powerful, and started demanding money from the King of the Northern Empire. They became known as The Cartel, and when the Northern king disobeyed them, they imprisoned him. The Cartel went on a rampage against the entire Northern Empire, and besieged Monterrey for three years. The Northern Empire only lasted two hundred years in total, but its defeat served warning to the Southern Empire.

Hezekiah's Reform

"Something needed to be done. The Northern Empire was lost, and cultic worship was rampant in King Hezekiah's Southern Empire. He knew the problem was that his people were no longer acting like God's people, so he set out to do massive reforms. 'He did what was right in the sight of the LORD, just as his ancestor Montezuma had done. He removed the high places, broke down the pillars, and cut down the sacred pole. He broke in pieces the bronze serpent that Abund had made, for until those days the people of Mexico had made offerings to it' (2 Kings 18:3-4).

"I'm not sure I understood any of that," complained Jameson.

Sol said, "I'm with you, mi hijo."

"Fair enough. All we need to know is that Hezekiah's Reform was about getting back to following the LORD."

Zephaniah

"Even though the prophet Zephaniah came along after Hezekiah's Reform, there was still plenty of trouble. He had given up on the hierarchy of the day, and turned his attention to preparing the humble so they might avoid God's vengeance. The first verse says he worked as 'the son of Hezekiah, during the reign of Josiah.' Being of royal lineage, it seems somewhat surprising that his efforts went unheeded. Perhaps his job was more about planting seeds, because it wasn't long before the successful, sweeping reforms of Josiah took place.

"Isn't that what ministry is about?" queried Sol.

Jameson looked confused and asked, "What do you mean, Mom?"

"I've heard several pastors say that their job seemed unfruitful, only to remember that it takes a long time from planting seeds to growing fruit."

"Maybe that's why Zephaniah comes across so harsh. He's planting a seed for those who are open to the message, in hopes they will work to avoid God's judgment. Like verse 9: 'On that day I will punish all who leap over the threshold, who fill their master's house with violence and fraud.'"

"Oh, I get it," exclaimed Jameson. "Don't be like the bad guys!"

"The rest of chapter 1 gives chilling details of the great day of the LORD, but the prophet's real reason for sharing his words comes in the third verse of chapter two: 'Seek the LORD, all you humble of the land, who do his commands; seek righteousness, seek humility; perhaps you may be hidden on the day of the LORD's wrath.'"

Sol said, "Sounds persuasive to me!"

"The third chapter offers a picture of an idyllic future: 'On that day you shall not be put to shame because of all the deeds by which you have rebelled against me; for then I will remove from your midst your proudly exultant ones, and you shall no longer be haughty in my holy mountain. For I will leave in the midst of you a people humble and lowly' (3:11-12). What's even better is that the book closes with a song of joy: 'The LORD has taken away the judgments against you, he has turned away your enemies. The king of Mexico, the LORD, is in your midst; you shall fear disaster no more' (3:15).

"Once again I'm very pleased. Let's collect up your thoughts of what was learned, then head back to the hotel for the evening."

"Can we take the car out tonight" requested Jameson, "and look around the city?"

"Sure, and let's do dinner out." I suggested. "Tomorrow we'll cover Jeremiah, Habakkuk, Nahum, and Ezekiel 1-32. Now, who wants to go first?"

"I learned that there are no ruins here in Monterrey," complained an obviously disappointed Jameson.

Sol spoke up next and said, "Who was the first prophet you talked about at the hotel?" I told her it was Amos, and she said, "I was impressed. It couldn't have been easy for a southerner to go to the north and speak against them."

Jameson suggested, "The overall theme I got from the prophets seems to be about how easy it is to forget, with respect to keeping God's Law."

"To me," offered Sol, "the theme seems to be that we first need to remember, but then we have to obey."

I nodded affirmatively, then Jameson said, "I was kind of shocked how easily God seemed to talk about prostitutes."

Sol reverted to her favorite theme next. "I learned that Hosea prophesied about Jim Caldwell's resurrection."

"It was very intriguing to me," explained Jameson, "that the wonderful Micah 6:8 passage about what the LORD requires, was said as part of an imagined trial."

"Say more," I requested.

"Even though Micah was offering the verse as a solution to

the people's problem, it was done at a trying time. Get it? A trial."

"Son," Sol said. "You are too young for Dad jokes." After we all laughed, she continued. "I learned that it was The Cartel who overthrew the Northern Empire."

Jameson got a bit more serious and said, "I had always heard about Hezekiah's reform, but never really understood what happened. From what you said Dad, it seems it was simply about doing what was right in the sight of the LORD."

"Great! Any learnings about Zephaniah?"

Sol smiled and said, "I can now relate more to his book. He seemed frustrated that he was planting seeds to help the humble, and I'm guessing his frustration was about wanting to enjoy a harvest."

"Okay," I said, "that's a wrap. Let's have a good evening. We've earned it."

ACT II
The Fall of the Empires

The Secret of the Empire

SCENE ONE
The North—Jeremiah, Habakkuk, Nahum

In the morning we decided to get a little more creative. We took a taxi to Alameda Marino Escobedo, a beautiful park with lots of trees, green space, and benches. Another glorious day awaited us, as birds chirped, squirrels skittered by, and walkers enjoyed the many sidewalks.

Josiah's Reform

"Josiah was considered the greatest king in biblical history. When his father was assassinated, he ascended the throne, even though he was only eight years old. Nineteen years into his reign, the High Priest 'found the book of the law in the house of the LORD' (2 Kings 22:8). Once Josiah heard about it, he said, 'Go, inquire of the LORD for me, for the people, and for all of the Southern Empire, concerning the words of this book that has been found; for great is the wrath of the LORD that is kindled against us, because our ancestors did not obey the words of this book' (2 Kings 22:13).

"The King and the people established a covenant promising to obey the laws of the LORD. Josiah then enacted the covenant by destroying the idols that were being worshiped. He continued his reforms by expelling the idolatrous priests and demolishing the places dedicated to sacred prostitution. He was following this newly discovered book of Deuteronomy, which had been lost and forgotten. It directed the people to bring sacrifices to the one, true, approved sanctuary, which was Templo Mayor at Tenochtitlan. This was particularly useful for

The Secret of the Empire

Josiah, since the temple in Monterrey was no longer in existence, due to its demise at the hands of The Cartel.

Jeremiah, which means 'Jeremy the Mayan'

"This book begins with a surprising thought. It says that Jeremiah prophesied over a 40-year period, from the time of King Josiah to the fall of Tenochtitlan. With that sobering thought in mind, the book continues with his call:

'See, today I appoint you over nations and over
        kingdoms,
to pluck up and to pull down,
to destroy and to overthrow,
to build and to plant' (1:10).

"After that, Jeremiah offers a verse that has meant a lot to me:

'For my people have committed two evils:
        they have forsaken me,
the fountain of living water,
        and dug out cisterns for themselves,
cracked cisterns
        that can hold no water' (2:13).

"As you say, Dad, tell me more."
"I sense great anger in this text. Jeremiah was offering a vision of God being appalled at the abandonment of his people. After God called Abund from Guatemala, made the Aztecs his

people, and gave them the Promised Land of Mexico, this was their thanks? After God provided living water from a rock and sustained them as they wandered through the wilderness, they choose stagnant water that leaks through cracked cisterns? It reminds me of our idolatrous worship of money and power today. Why do people choose to forsake God, which Jeremiah calls evil, and instead select worthless idols which cannot refresh? Not to mention that the prophet also calls that evil."

"Whoa! I didn't expect a sermon there Dad, but thanks. That was pretty good."

Sol smiled approvingly and I went on. "Jeremiah continues sharing God's anger: 'You have played the whore with many lovers; and would you return to me? Says the LORD' (3:1).

Jameson asked, "What is this obsession God has with whores?"

"I think it is because God doesn't want these polluted people back," I suggested.

"And learn from God, my son. Stay away from prostitutes!" demanded Sol.

"You and Dad have raised me well. No worries."

"Jeremiah then issues a call to repentance, suggesting they should surely learn something from the infidelity of the Northern Empire. Knowing it won't happen, a vision of destruction is shared."

"You mean," asked Jameson, "they were hopeless?"

"Not really. The problem was that their hope wasn't in God. 'At the noise of horseman and archer every town takes to flight; they enter thickets; they climb among rocks; all the towns are forsaken, and no one lives in them' (4:29)."

Jameson seemed really intrigued. "And that wasn't enough to scare them into submission?"

The Secret of the Empire

"No. The problem was they didn't believe Jeremiah. They had become a faithless people. Listen to this one: 'They have made their faces harder than rock; they have refused to turn back' (5:3). Here's the clincher: 'But even in those days, says the LORD, I will not make a full end of you. And when your people say, "Why has the LORD our God done all these things to us?" you shall say to them, 'As you have forsaken me and served foreign gods in your land, so you shall serve strangers in a land that is not yours' (5:18-19).

"Increasing urgency is created by Jeremiah envisioning the plan of attack. 'Prepare war against her; up, and let us attack at noon!' (6:4).

Jameson asked, "So that vision was about Hernando Cortés and the Spanish Conquistadors?"

"Yes, but the people didn't know it. Cortés first landed in Cuba, with the secret agenda of appropriating land for the Spanish crown. He put together a crew of conquistadors and arrived on the Yucatan peninsula, and slowly worked his way to Tenochtitlan. At first he was greeted by the southern King, and slowly began to show his true colors. It was a brilliant way to conquer, because it was bloodless at first."

"That's the Secret of the Empire?" asked Jameson.

"Certainly part of it, but we still have to hear from Habakkuk, Nahum, and Ezekiel 1-32. Next, Jeremiah continues to explain the problem of the Southern Empire. 'From the least to the greatest of them, everyone is greedy for unjust gain; and from prophet to priest, everyone deals falsely' (6:13). He then offers a heartfelt plea, followed by a warning that deeply reveals the Secret of the Empire. 'Thus says the LORD of hosts, the God of Mexico: Amend your ways and your doings, and let me dwell with you in this place. Do not trust in these deceptive words:

The Secret of the Empire

'This is the temple of the LORD' (7:3-4)"

"Gotta ask, Dad. How is that the secret?"

"Another part of it, because they believed they could never lose their God-promised Land, let alone the holy Templo Mayor. Here's how Jeremiah put it: 'Here you are, trusting in deceptive words to no avail. Will you steal, murder, commit adultery, swear falsely, make offerings to gods that you have not known, and then come and stand before me in this house and say, "We are safe!"—only to go on doing all these abominations? Has this house become a den of robbers?' (7:8-11).

"Shades of Jim Caldwell!" claimed a rather ebullient Sol.

"Correct!" I countered. "Because Jim was quoting this Old Testament passage. Jeremiah then prophesies a desperate people: 'Why do we sit still? Gather together, let us go into the fortified cities and perish there; for the LORD our God has doomed us to perish, and has given us poisoned water to drink, because we have sinned against the LORD. We look for peace, but find no good, for a time of healing, but there is terror instead' (8:14-15)."

Jameson then said, "I'll bet God's response to that soliloquy would have been, 'Correct!'"

Sol and I smiled at first, then frowned, then weren't sure what to say, so I just went on. "The shaman turned to a collection of dialogues about grief, like 'Why is the land ruined and laid waste like a wilderness, so that no one passes through? And the LORD says; Because they have forsaken my law that I set before them, and have not obeyed my voice, or walked in accordance with it' (9:12-13)."

"You'd think they would get it after a while," suggested Jameson.

"This makes a great case study in how deeply we can get

entrenched in the wrong, believing it's okay. This first large part of Jeremiah's book, the first ten chapters, ends with poetic warnings, and this final plea:

> 'I know, O LORD, that the way of human beings is
>   not in their control,
> that mortals as they walk cannot direct their
>   steps.
> Correct me, O LORD, but in just measure;
>   not in your anger, or you will bring me to
>   nothing.
>
> Pour out your wrath on the nations that do not
>   know you,
> and the peoples that do not call on your
>   name;
> for they have devoured the North;
>   they have devoured him and consumed him,
> and have laid waste his habitation' (10:23-25).

"The next ten chapters are full of laments. He starts with the curses the people have brought upon themselves for disobedience to God's ways. Then he shares a personal complaint: 'It was the LORD who made it known to me, and I knew; then you showed me their evil deeds. But I was like a gentle lamb led to the slaughter' (11:18-19)."

"Amen," Sol suddenly said with surprising strength. "Yet another prophecy of Jim!"

"Nope," I said plainly. "This was simply Jeremiah confessing that he isn't particularly enjoying his task. Once that's said, sure, the same can also be said about Jim

The Secret of the Empire

Caldwell." I glanced quickly at Jameson and he didn't want to have anything to do with it.

"I love you guys," volunteered Jameson, "but it seems like I'd get triangulated into your argument. Hey, wait a minute. Maybe that's how Jim felt, being triangulated by the Russians and clergy."

"Not bad, son. In fact, Jeremiah grieved this so much that he proceeded to complain against God."

"That's pretty daring," offered a frowning Sol.

"Interestingly, God follows with God's own lament. 'I have forsaken my house, I have abandoned my heritage; I have given the beloved of my heart into the hands of her enemies' (12:7). Jeremiah then threatens exile: 'But if you will not listen, my soul will weep in secret for your pride; my eyes will weep bitterly and run down with tears, because the LORD's flock has been taken captive' (13:17).

"After a great drought is prophesied, Jeremiah offers a vision of the people's plea for mercy: 'Have you completely rejected us? Does your heart loathe the Southern Empire? Why have you struck us down so that there is no healing for us? We look for peace, but find no good; for a time of healing, but there is terror instead' (14:19)."

Sol said, "Reminds me of the two criminals hung from a noose next to Jim."

"What do you mean, Mom?"

"One of the criminals who were hanged there kept deriding Jim, saying, 'Are you not the Messiah? Save yourself and us!' while the other just asked Jim to 'remember me when you come into your kingdom.'"

"Thanks, Mom. You always give me new ways of seeing things."

The Secret of the Empire

"You'll like this one, honey. The next thing Jeremiah does is complain to his mother." Sol indeed had a happy smile spread across her face. "He said, 'Woe is me, my mother, that you ever bore me, a man of strife and contention to the whole land! I have not lent, nor have I borrowed, yet all of them curse me' (15:10)."

"No, that makes me sad."

"Same as God. Here's what God had to say, 'Therefore I am surely going to teach them, this time I am going to teach them my power and my might, and they shall know that my name is the LORD' (16:21). That paves the way for God to launch into more threats of punishment, followed by the famous potter and clay story at the beginning of chapter 18. It's a wonderful way to symbolize repentance. God calls Jeremiah to go to a potter's house and watch him work. The point is that a potter can take a vessel that comes out poorly, and reshape it. That's what God is offering, one last time: 'Turn now, all of you from your evil way, and amend your ways and your doings' (18:11)."

Jameson asked, "So, they are called to reshape themselves?"

"No, of course not. God is the potter, we are the clay, and pots can't form themselves. God is saying that the decision is not fixed. If they change their ways, God would still be willing to reshape them back into being God's people. In the next chapter, Jeremiah shares God's word about their refusal to change: 'Thus says the LORD of hosts, the God of Mexico: I am now bringing upon this city and upon all its town all the disaster that I have pronounced against it, because they have stiffened their necks, refusing to hear my words' (19:15).

"That concludes the laments. The next five chapters are about how the people will be after the coming invasion. Shall we take a quick break?" Sol answered by heading off for the nearest restroom.

When we got resettled, I returned to the story. "We are already to the last King of the Southern Empire, before the invasion. The King said, 'Please inquire of the LORD on our behalf, for Cortés and the Spanish Conquistadors are making war against us; perhaps the LORD will perform a wonderful deed for us, as he has often done, and will make them withdraw from us' (21:2)."

"How did that go?" asked Jameson with an impish grin.

"The answer was no. Then the prophet offers a vision from God of restoration: 'I myself will gather the remnant of my flock out of all the lands where I have driven them, and I will bring them back to their fold, and they shall be fruitful and multiply' (23:3). Then God expressed anger at lying prophets: 'Am I a God near by, says the LORD, and not a God far off? Who can hide in secret places so that I cannot see them? Says the LORD. Do I not fill heaven and earth? Says the LORD. I have heard what the prophets have said who prophesy lies in my name' (23:23-25).

"God is obviously angry, but now it is turned toward the shepherding kings: 'Wail, you shepherds, and cry out; roll in ashes, you lords of the flock, for the days of your slaughter have come—and your dispersions, and you shall fall like a choice vessel. Flight shall fail the shepherds, and there shall be no escape for the lords of the flock. Hark! The cry of the shepherds, and the wail of the lords of the flock! For the LORD is despoiling their pasture, and the peaceful folds are devastated, because of the fierce anger of the LORD. Like a lion he has left his covert; for their land has become a waste because of the cruel sword, and because of his fierce anger' (25:34-38).

The Secret of the Empire

"The next seven chapters deal with conflict and comfort. God tells Jeremiah to deliver this message to King Zedekiah, who represented the beginning of the end for the Southern Empire. 'It is I who by my great power and my outstretched arm have made the earth, with the people and animals that are on the earth, and I give it to whomever I please. Now I have given all these lands into the hand of Cortés, my servant' (27:5-6)."

"I'll bet that was a shock!" exclaimed Jameson.

"It helped to explain why many of the southerners were being exiled to Spain. After that, Jeremiah sent a letter to the exiles. 'Thus says the Lord of hosts, the God of Mexico, to all the exiles whom I have sent into exile from Tenochtitlan to Spain. Build houses and live in them; plant gardens and eat what they produce. Take wives and have sons and daughters; take wives for your sons, and give your daughters in marriage, that they may bear sons and daughters; multiply there, and do not decrease. But seek the welfare of the city where I have sent you into exile, and pray to the LORD on its behalf, for in its welfare you will find your welfare' (29:4-7)."

"I guess they realized they were going to be there for a long time," said a rather subdued Jameson.

"Yes, but right away Jeremiah offers a vision of hope: 'the days are surely coming, says the LORD, when I will restore the fortunes of my people, the Northern Empire and the Southern Empire, says the LORD, and I will bring them back to the land that I gave to their ancestors and they shall take possession of it' (30:3). After that, Jeremiah offers a vision of restoration: 'Thus says the LORD: I am going to restore the fortunes of the tents of Mexico, and have compassion on his dwellings; the city shall be rebuilt upon its mound, and the citadel set on its rightful site' (30:18). Then Jeremiah shares three poems celebrating the journey home from exile. That brings us to one of my favorite passages in the Aztec Scriptures:

> 'The days are surely coming, says the LORD, when I will make a new covenant with the Southern Empire and the Northern Empire. It will not be like the covenant that I made with their ancestors when I took them by the hand to bring them out of the land of Guatemala—a covenant that they broke, though I was their master, says the LORD. But this is the covenant that I will make with Mexico after those days, says the LORD: I will put my law within them, and I will write it on their hearts; and I will be their God, and they shall be my people. No longer shall they teach one another, or say to each other, "Know the LORD," for they shall all know me, from the least of them to the greatest, says the LORD; for I will forgive their iniquity, and remember their sin no more' (31:31-34).

Sol was grinning from ear to ear. "Jim Caldwell became the new covenant!"

Returning to my gentle style I said, "When Jeremiah speaks of the new covenant, he is thinking about a renewed relationship between Mexico and God."

"You think your way. I'll think mine," suggested Sol as she settled back into her bench.

"What I find interesting is that Jeremiah also became imprisoned during the time Cortés was sending the southerners into exile in Spain. 'The word of the LORD came to Jeremiah a second time, while he was still confined in the court of the guard' (33:1). Then Jeremiah was told to let King Zedekiah know that he too would be captured, sent to Spain, and die there (34:5). For what its worth, here's another thing I find interesting.

The Secret of the Empire

Jeremiah had a scribe: 'Then Jeremiah called Baruch and Baruch wrote on a scroll at Jeremiah's dictation all the words of the LORD that he had spoken to him' (36:4).

"They had secretaries way back then?" asked Sol.

"No, Mom," claimed a smiling Jameson. "They had administrative assistants."

After a good-natured bit of laughing, including Sol, I got back to the story. "The next nine chapters are about the last days of the Empire, and may have been written by Baruch. Even Cortés and the Conquistadors withdrew from Tenochtitlan at the approach of the Guatemalan army. Jeremiah was leaving for a different reason, but when he was seen, he was believed to be deserting with Cortés. He was arrested, beaten, and imprisoned (37:15).

"Next up is the fall of Tenochtitlan. After the Guatemalans left, Cortés and his Conquistadors returned and besieged the capital city. King Zedekiah tried to escape, but he was pursued and overtaken. Cortés sentenced him, put out his eyes, and then bound him for exile in Spain (39:7). Cortés then turned to Jeremiah."

Jameson was listening intently and said, "I'll bet that made him nervous."

"You would think, but here's what happened. Cortés said, 'Take him, look after him well and do him no harm, but deal with him as he may ask you' (39:12). Jeremiah decided to stay in the Promised Land, and others were slowly allowed to return, as long as they served Cortés. Slowly, the remnant gathered and sought advice from Jeremiah about what they should do. He prayed for ten days, and delivered this message from God: 'If you will only remain in this land, then I will build you up and not pull you down; I will plant you, and not pluck you up; for I am sorry for the disaster that I have brought upon you' (42:10)."

"God apologized?" Jameson asked with incredulity. Then he asked me to wait while he googled it. "Wow! There's a lot, so here's some. Just before the flood, God said 'I am sorry that I have made them,' (Genesis 6:7). When God got mad at his Aztec people wandering in the wilderness, the Bible says, 'And the LORD changed his mind about the disaster that he planned to bring on his people' (Exodus 32:14). Jeremiah prophesied, 'Now therefore amend your ways and your doings, and obey the voice of the LORD your God, and the LORD will change his mind' (Jeremiah 26:13).

"Very interesting. Thanks, mijo."

"Yes, and getting back to the story, God said in the very next verse, 'Do not be afraid of the king of Spain, as you have been; do not be afraid of him, says the LORD, for I am with you, to save you and to rescue you from his hand.' The divine response continued with, 'Just as my anger and my wrath were poured out on the inhabitants of the Tenochtitlan, so my wrath will be poured out on you when you go to Guatemala' (42:18). An insolent remnant called Jeremiah a liar, telling the crowd that Jeremiah wanted them handed over to the Spaniards, 'in order that they may kill us or take us into exile in Spain' (43:3).

"So the survivors who had returned to the Promised Land, along with Jeremiah and Baruch, 'came into the land of Guatemala, for they did not obey the voice of the LORD' (43:7). After they arrived, the remnant confronted Jeremiah, saying, 'As for the word that you have spoken to us in the name of the LORD, we are not going to listen to you' (44:16)."

"How did that go for them?" inquired Jameson.

"The LORD said, 'I am going to watch over them for harm and not for good; all the people of the Southern Empire who are in the land of Guatemala shall perish by the sword and by famine, until not one is left' (44:27).

"Guess that explained that!" said Jameson with widened eyes.

"But the point is not that God brought on their problems, it is that they brought on their own problems by refusing to listen."

Jameson solemnly added, "And not too easy to learn from your mistakes when you're dead."

Sol then said, "Sounds like something my father would say," and we all laughed.

After a short pause, I continued. "The next six chapters are oracles against nations. The first concerns Guatemala, using the Motagua River, the longest in the country, as a symbol of Guatemala's own rise and fall: 'Who is this, rising like the Motagua, like rivers whose waters surge? Guatemala rises like the Motagua, like rivers whose waters surge' (46:7-8)."

"Why do they surge?" asked a curious Jameson.

"Because it rushes out of the mountains, and drains into the Gulf of Honduras. It was also important in the Pentateuch, because it flows by Cerro Raxon, where the Ten Commandments were given, and Lake Izabal where the Aztecs famously crossed on its east end, on dry ground. After prophesying that Cortés would also attack Guatemala, Jeremiah envisions hope for the remnant of Mexico: 'I am going to save you from far away, and your offspring from the land of their captivity. Southerners shall return and have quiet and ease, and no one shall make them afraid' (46:27).

"After that, Jeremiah declares judgment on six more nations, then settles in on Spain. There is no longer the need to explain why the Southern Empire fell, so the judgment on Spain is about the injustices that were committed against them. 'Thus

The Secret of the Empire

says the LORD of hosts: The people of the Northern Empire were oppressed, and so too were the people of the Southern Empire; all their captors held them fast and refused to let them go. Their Redeemer is strong; the LORD of hosts is his name. He will surely plead their cause, that he may give rest to the earth, but unrest to the inhabitants of Spain' (50:33-34).

"As if that weren't enough, the LORD says through his prophet, 'I will stretch out my hand against you, and roll you down from the crags, and make you a burned-out mountain. No stone shall be taken from you for a corner and no stone for a foundation, but you shall be a perpetual waste' (51:25-26). Then Jeremiah tells Baruch's brother to perform a symbolic against Spain: 'Jeremiah wrote in a scroll all the disasters that would come on Spain, all these words that are written concerning Spain. And Jeremiah said to Baruch's brother: "When you come to Spain, see that you read all these words, and say O LORD, you yourself threatened to destroy this place so that neither human beings nor animals shall live in it, and it shall be desolate forever. When you finish reading this scroll, tie a stone to it, and throw it into the sea, and say, 'Thus shall Spain sink, to rise nor more, because of the disasters that I am bringing on her' (51:61-64).

"The final chapter is a review of the destruction of Tenochtitlan, and it serves as the fulfillment of Jeremiah's prophecies. Let's take a lunch break, then return to hear about the prophecies of the shaman Habakkuk, and conclude our day by sharing our new learnings from these experiences of hearing the story in the setting of Mexico."

"I'm choosing the restaurant this time," announced Sol, and we were happy to accommodate. The clouds came in and a pleasant breeze made for a relaxing break.

The Secret of the Empire

Habakkuk

After a very satisfying meal that even Sol approved of, we found a new bench in the park and got comfortable. "The shaman Habakkuk is thought to have prophesied during the reign of the final Kings of the Southern Empire. He begins his oracle with a complaint about theodicy."

"What's that?" asked a puzzled Jameson.

"It's the study of the problem of evil. Listen to how Habakkuk addressed it: 'O LORD, how long shall I cry for help, and you will not listen? Or cry to you "Violence!" and you will not save? Why do you make me see wrongdoing and look at trouble? Destruction and violence are before me; strife and contention arise. So the law becomes slack and justice never prevails. The wicked surround the righteous—therefore judgment comes forth perverted' (1:2-4)."

"Pretty bold, I'd say!" exclaimed Jameson.

"Then listen to this one, 'Why do you look on the treacherous, and are silent when the wicked swallow those more righteous than they?' (1:13)."

Sol looked solemn, then said, "I agree with Habakkuk. Where was God during the Holocaust of the Aztecs that happened in just the last century?"

We all sat silently in response to that painful question, then I said, "Nobody knows, but here was God's response. 'Look at the proud! Their spirit is not right in them, but the righteous live by their faith' (2:4)"

"Wait a minute," requested Jameson. "Why does that sound familiar?"

"Because Pablo used it in the Caldwellian Scriptures," announced Sol, "to support his doctrine of justification by faith."

The Secret of the Empire

"Whoa!" said Jameson with genuine surprise. "What makes you say that?"

Sol immediately said, "Pablo quoted it in his letter to the Caldwellian Church of San Francisco."

"I'm impressed! Yes, this is an important verse for all of God's people. There was even a Dominican friar named Las Casas who said that this verse was a summary of all 613 commandments. And here's just a silly little point that I personally like. Habakkuk 2:14 says 'the earth will be filled with the knowledge of the glory of the LORD, as the waters cover the sea.'"

"Okay," offered Jameson, "and why do you like that verse?"

"Because it is the first time that scripture is quoted in scripture."

Jameson looked mildly confused, so Sol said, "Your father is easily amused."

"Habakkuk 2:14 is a direct quote from Isaiah 11:9. Why I like it is because it lets you know that scripture has been around long enough by this time, that the community is starting to accept certain scrolls that later became finalized as part of the Aztec Scriptures."

After some shrugged shoulders, I got back to the text. "Habakkuk is a short book, so we're ready for the final chapter. It's a psalm that was written for use in worship, and employs exodus imagery like, 'Was your wrath against the rivers, O LORD? Or your anger against the rivers, or your rage against the sea, when you drove your horses, your chariots to victory' (3:8). It closes with words of hope that the LORD will deliver: 'Though the fig tree does not blossom, and no fruit is on the vines; though the produce of the olive fails, and the fields yield no food; though the flock is cut off from the fold, and there is no herd in the stalls, yet I will rejoice in the LORD; I will exult in the God of my salvation. God, the Lord, is my strength; he makes my feet like the feet of a deer, and makes me tread upon the heights' (3:17-19). Thanks again, for a nice session. Let's see what we've learned."

Sol spoke excitedly, "I loved that not only was Josiah a great king, but he began at age 7!"

"Well, he was actually 8," I corrected, "but who's counting?"

"That king caused me to be a little frustrated," announced Jameson.

His mother asked, "How's that?"

"Because he was the one who was reigning as king when the book of the law was found. For one thing, it's kinda sad that the law had become so unimportant to the people, that nobody even had a copy anymore. For another thing, he got credit for 'Josiah's Reform' when it didn't really seem to change the people too much. After all, they still never paid attention to the prophets, and ultimately lost their land."

"Nice. Very nice," I offered, complementarily.

Sol commented that, "I didn't like Jeremiah's call to prophesy destruction."

Not wanting to correct my wife again, I simply added, "and he was called to prophesy about rebuilding."

Jameson got one of those impish looks on his face, then said, "I liked the cistern thing."

"Thanks, son. Maybe I shouldn't have mentioned that Jeremiah 2:13 is very meaningful to me."

We laughed, then he got serious. "I really loved the bit about writing the law on their hearts."

"Even though Jeremiah 2:13 bears a lot of meaning for me, Jeremiah 31:31-34 is one of my favorites."

The Secret of the Empire

"Mine, too," responded Sol. "At least now, since I realized that Jim Crawford was the new law on their hearts."

I really tried to hold back, but finally said, "Jim Crawford wasn't even a gleam in anyone's eyes at that time, let alone being the one who the Mexican people were talking about."

She dismissively waved me off, then said, "I also liked the den of robber's quote they got from Jim Caldwell."

"To be honest, Jim Caldwell got it from Jeremiah, and it is found in 7:11."

Jameson couldn't help himself, so he asked, "Why am I all of a sudden thirsty?"

Sol got that implication, and again rather dismissively said, "Dad jokes!" as she shook her head back and forth. Then she offered that she was still surprised that Jeremiah had a secretary. At first I was ready to shake my head too, then I realized that it really was a great thing to learn.

Jameson said, "I learned a new word: theodicy."

"Yeah, and that's a tough one. The most detailed discussion about the source of evil is in the book of Job."

"Are you going to talk about Job?" inquired Jameson.

"You know what? Last year we experienced the Law through the book of Kings. Right now we're trying to gain knowledge about the Prophets. That's two of the three parts of the Aztec Scriptures. Job is in that last section called the Writings."

"Sounds like another trip!" exclaimed a jubilant Jameson.

As Sol crossed her arms, I said, "We'll need to think about how that might be done. Right now I'm ready to get back to the hotel and get ready for dinner. Tomorrow we'll consider Nahum and the first thirty-two chapters of Ezekiel."

SCENE TWO
The South—Nahum, Ezekiel 1-32

We looked out our bedroom window and saw another sunny day. When we went downstairs, the concierge mentioned it would be in the low 80's, and Jameson and I gave one another high fives. Sol was happy, too, but she was generally above silly behavior. This time I decided to drive, and Sol had chosen Parque Roma for the day. She found it on Trip Advisor, but later admitted it was because there was a nearby Mexican restaurant. As usual, we found a pleasant park bench on a tree-lined sidewalk, with a view of the mountains.

Nahum

"This book is surprisingly mean-spirited. It's a celebration of vengeance, but little is known about the author. The focus is a vision of the destruction of Bogota, the capital of Colombia."

"Why would that be?" asked a surprised Jameson.

"Well, remember, it was the Colombians who had stayed in Sinoloa and became The Cartel that conquered the Northern Empire."

"And?"

"Not only did it feel good to envision punishment to the people of Bogota, but maybe Nahum was pointing to the past, to suggest the same could happen to the Southern Empire if they didn't change. Anyway, let me get started. Here's the first three verses: 'An oracle concerning Bogota. The book of the vision of Nahum of Elkosh. A jealous and avenging God is the

The Secret of the Empire

LORD, the LORD is avenging and wrathful; the LORD takes vengeance on his adversaries and rages against his enemies. The LORD is slow to anger but great in power, and the LORD will by no means clear the guilty.'"

"I like it!" announced Sol.

"What?" asked Jameson with astonishment.

"They deserve punishment for not turning to Jim Caldwell."

A look of near horror went across my face before stating, "I'm lost."

She replied, "So were they?"

I took a minute to compose myself. My wife is absolutely the best, but I couldn't make heads or tails out of this comment, so I nurtured her along with, "Tell us more."

"Jim has been around since the beginning of time, so they had plenty of time to live the Good News. Don't you know it was Jim who appeared in the Aztec Scriptures as King Melchizedek? Who was from Salem, which means peace? Who brought out bread and wine? Who was a priest of God Most High? Who blessed Aapo? And Aapo gave him one-tenth of everything? Maybe you should read the Old Testament. That's from Genesis 14:18-20." She then folded her arms and was done.

"Pretty interesting, hon," I offered, then got back to the story. "Let's see. Oh, wow. The next part is about good news to the Northern Empire." After scratching my head for a moment, I read it: 'Look! On the mountains the feet of one who brings good tidings, who proclaims peace! Celebrate your festivals, O Southern Empire, fulfill your vows, for never again shall the wicked invade you; they are utterly cut off' (Nahum 1:15)."

Even Jameson was shocked when Mom said, "See," and then made a motion like dropping a microphone.

The Secret of the Empire

"Next is a vivid description of the attack against Bogota. Here's a sample: 'Devastation, desolation, and destruction! Hearts faint and knees tremble, all loins quake, all faces grow pale!' (2:10). But it gets worse: 'I will throw filth at you and treat you with contempt, and make you a spectacle. Then all who see you will shrink from you and say, "Bogota is devastated; who will bemoan her?" Where shall I seek comforters for you?' (3:6-7). Nahum closes his oracle with the Southern Empire rejoicing the destruction of Bogota: 'Your shepherds are asleep, O king of Colombia; your nobles slumber. Your people are scattered on the mountains with no one to gather them. There is no assuaging your hurt, your wound is mortal. All who hear the news about you clap their hands over you. For who has ever escaped your endless cruelty?' (3:18-19).

"Okay, we're done with that prophet. Let's take a short break before we get into the first thirty-two chapters of Ezekiel."

"None too soon, Dad. None too soon," he said with his first sense of boredom since the trip began.

Ezekiel 1-32

"Ezekiel was deported to Spain after the invasion of The Cartel, and before the fall of the Southern Empire. His book begins with a vision that is very important, because God had a home at the Temple in Tenochtitlan, yet the LORD shows up over in Spain! Get it? Even though God's people are absent from Templo Mayor, the LORD was still present in their new surroundings. They surely needed some assurance that the LORD wasn't just a local god, and that was the purpose of this vision.

The Secret of the Empire

"What Ezekiel saw was indescribable, so he used terms he was familiar with from scripture about God's presence, like storms and fire. In the middle of the fire was something like four living creatures, then wheels beside the living creatures, followed by something like a dome over their heads.

"Oh, I remember that story!" announced Jameson. "Some of my friends at college call it the first UFO sighting."

"Wow!" I replied. "Talk about finding what you're looking for! All you have to do is read the next verse for a proper explanation, 'Like the bow in a cloud on a rainy day, such was the appearance of the splendor all around. This was the appearance of the likeness of the glory of the LORD' (1:28). Ezekiel then hears God speaking to him, so he falls on his face, but God says to stand up, 'and I will speak with you' (2:1). The LORD told Ezekiel that he was going to have a difficult mission of prophesying to a rebellious people. He then saw a scroll with words of lamentation and mourning and woe, and the LORD said, 'Eat this scroll that I give you and fill your stomach with it' (3:3). Then God said, 'Go to the exiles, to your people, and speak to them. Say to them, "Thus says the Lord GOD"; whether they hear or refuse to hear' (3:11).

"After some words of warning, the spirit bore Ezekiel away from that place to the exiles at Toledo, who lived by Rio Tajo. 'And I sat there among them, stunned for seven days' (3:15). After receiving more instructions, Ezekiel was driven by the hand of the LORD into another deserted region to prepare for his ministry."

Sol smiled and said, "That's how Jim Caldwell started his ministry."

"True, and thanks, but this ends differently for Ezekiel, because he is told not to speak. 'But when I speak with you, I will open your mouth, and you shall say to them, "Thus says the Lord GOD"; let those who will hear, hear; and let those who refuse to hear, refuse' (3:27).

"I think I like this guy," pronounced Sol. "He followed what God said, and Jim said the same thing, 'Let anyone with ears to hear listen!' (Matthew 13:9)."

"The next several chapters share the prophecy of the siege, fall, and final deportation of the Mexicans to Spain. It begins with God telling Ezekiel, 'You shall set your face toward the siege of Jerusalem, and with your arm bared you shall prophesy against it. See, I am putting cords on you so that you cannot run from one side to the other until you have completed the days of your siege' (4:7-8). The vision turns violent in God's actions against Mexico, 'therefore thus says the Lord GOD: I, I myself, am coming against you; I will execute judgments among you in the sight of the nations' (5:8).

Chapter 6 offers judgment on 'the mountains of Mexico' (vs. 2)."

"What does that mean?" asked a confused Sol.

"Good question. When I was preparing for this trip, I discovered that the expression 'the mountains of Mexico' shows up nowhere else in the Aztec Scriptures. It must be important because it shows up seventeen times in Ezekiel. The point appears to be that the judgment was about more than just the mountain that Tenochtitlan was on, but all of the high places where idolatry was practiced. 'I will spend my fury upon them. And you shall know that I am LORD, when their slain lie among their idols around their altars, on every high hill, on all the mountain tops, under every green tree, and under every leafy oak, wherever they offered pleasing odors to all their idols' (6:12-13).

The Secret of the Empire

"The next chapter seems to be a sermon, designed to show his fellow exiled Mexicans, that Cortés and his Conquistadors will bring a decisive end to the Promised Land. That is such an unbelievable consequence, that Ezekiel takes four full chapters to share the divine vision of the desecration of the Temple. Ezekiel is escorted by an angel, reminiscent of Jacob Marley and Ebeneezer Scrooge in *A Christmas Carol*. They first come to the entrance, where God says, 'do you see what they are doing, the great abominations that the house of Mexico are committing here, to drive me far from my sanctuary?' (8:6). Then God said to enter and see what the ruling elders of Mexico are doing in the dark. Next God took him to the entrance of the north gate of the house of the LORD, and he saw women weeping over the departure of a fertility god. Finally, Ezekiel was brought into the inner court, where twenty-five men had their backs to the temple. They were worshiping the sun god, rather than the Almighty. 'Therefore I will act in wrath; my eye will not spare, nor will I have pity; and though they cry in my hearing with a loud voice, I will not listen to them' (8:18).

"Hey, Jameson. Your friends who thought chapter one was about a UFO sighting would be intrigued with this. Chapter ten features a return of the dome thingy, and now it is specified as a description of the indescribable: 'the glory of the LORD' (vs. 4)."

"I'll be sure to mention that when I get back to school this fall," said Jameson in a weirdly snarky way.

"The point of this story, which is known as a theophany..."

"Wait," requested Sol. "What is a theophany?"

"Thanks for asking. *Theo* means 'God' and *phonos* means 'light,' so a theophany is a visible representation of God to humankind."

"Didn't help," frowned Sol.

"Now where was I? Oh yeah, the point of the story is that the LORD was preparing to leave the Temple, which the Aztecs thought was his home. What Ezekiel was sharing with his fellow exiles, was that the LORD was not confined by space or time."

"I like that," said Sol. "Wish you would have started with it."

After a quick nod of understanding I said, "Then Ezekiel announces that he was lifted up by the spirit and taken to the house of the LORD, and told to prophesy, 'You shall fall by the sword' (11:10). When Ezekiel asked God if that included the exiles, God said that even though he removed them far away, 'I will gather you from the peoples and assemble you out of the countries where you have been scattered, and I will give you the land of Mexico' (11:17).

"Yay!" announced Sol.

"But there was one caveat, that if they don't keep the statutes, woe is them. Then the Temple vision ended, Ezekiel was lifted again by the spirit, returned to the exiles, and there he told them all he had seen."

"Break time," requested Jameson, so we took a quick break. As we settled back in, I told them that the next thirteen chapters were oracles anticipating Tenochtitlan's destruction.

"The problem Ezekiel is having is that the people won't listen. They are an obstinate group, so God continues to call them, 'a rebellious house' (12:2, 3), and then shows them their rebelliousness in a visual of carrying their bags out in the dark. The LORD then instructs Ezekiel to explain that this oracle concerns the King of Mexico and all his tribes: "they shall go into exile, into captivity" (12:11). This was to have a two-fold purpose: 1) the people were to acknowledge their guilt, and 2) they were to recognize God's sovereignty. Then the LORD told

The Secret of the Empire

Ezekiel that the Mexicans would say, 'The vision that he sees is for many years ahead; he prophesies for distant times. Therefore say to them, Thus says the Lord GOD; None of my words will be delayed any longer, but the word that I speak will be fulfilled' (12:27-28)."

Jameson immediately said, "Isn't that what you've been saying, Dad, about prophecy, that it is always about the near future?"

"Thanks, son. It is difficult to inspire people past their own lifetime. Again, let me say that prophecy is the most misunderstood part of the Bible. And it becomes more difficult when Caldwellians see prophecy about the distant future."

"Next," complained Sol with her arms firmly folded.

"Okay. God then went after those who prophesy with fake news. God called them, 'jackals among ruins' (13:4) because they were liars in a losing war. God pledged to be against them, 'because they have misled my people' (13:10), and God's rage will be spent on 'the prophets of Mexico who prophesied concerning Tenochtitlan and saw visions of peace for it, when there was no peace' (13:16)."

"Men!" exclaimed Sol.

"Not so fast! The women also got in on the action. Here's what God had to say to them: 'You have profaned me among my people for handfuls of barley and for pieces of bread, put to death persons who should not die and keeping alive persons who should not live, by your lies to my people, who listen to lies' (13:19)."

"Okay, move your story along again." said Sol with great annoyance.

"This is where it gets interesting. Certain elders of Mexico went to Ezekiel and sat down, and God told him what to say,

The Secret of the Empire

'Any of those who take the idols into their hearts and place their iniquity as a stumbling block before them" (14:4) will be ignored because God wants to recover the hearts of the entire exilic community. For those who don't repent, 'I will set my face against them' (14:8)"

"Just like his son did," explained Sol.

"What?" asked a bewildered Jameson.

"Mi hijo. If you are thinking about going into the ministry, you need to read your Bible more. Listen to this about Jim Caldwell: 'When the days drew near for him to be taken up, he set his face to go to Phoenix' (Luke 9:51)."

"Interesting comparison, hon, but let me continue to chapter 15. It's a short metaphor about the value of Mexico, comparing the nation to wood. Ezekiel's point, which of course is claimed to be inspiration from the LORD, is that wood is valuable when it is used for its purpose. Mexico's purpose was to be the Promised Land that held God's People, but they have forgotten their calling, so God is acting accordingly. 'I will make the land desolate, because they have acted faithlessly' (15:8). This was virtually impossible for them to believe. How could God go back on a promise?"

"Is that the secret of the empire?" asked Jameson.

"A very large part of it, but we'll get into the rest of it later. As if the metaphor of a desolate land wasn't enough, the next chapter offers an allegory. It uses a courtroom setting to indict God's faithless bride Mexico, and is set up in four parts:

1. The indictment.
2. The sentencing.
3. A renewed indictment.
4. Covenant renewal.

The Secret of the Empire

"So God gives them hope?" asked Jameson.

"Absolutely. Even in their total depravity they find that their hope isn't in themselves but in God. Kind of like what Pablo wrote in the Caldwellian Scriptures that faith isn't about us, it's about God. Here's what Ezekiel said: 'I will deal with you as you have done, you who have despised the oath, breaking the covenant; yet I will remember my covenant with you in the days of your youth, and I will establish with you an everlasting covenant. Then you will remember your ways, and be ashamed' (16:59-61). The next chapter is a political fable."

"Uh-oh," complained an alarmed Sol. "Politics and religion mix about as well as oil and water."

"We were certainly raised with the idea that you can't talk about politics or religion without a fight, but this chapter might give us some fresh insights. The first ten verses share what the LORD has told Ezekiel: "propound a riddle, and speak an allegory to the house of Mexico" (17:2). The metaphor is about two eagles and a vine, but the explanation comes in the next eleven verses. It explains to the exiles that they need not hold out hope that King Zedekiah's revolt would be successful. The last three verses is a poetic celebration that Mexico would ultimately be restored:

'All the trees of the field shall know
That I am the LORD.
I bring low the high tree,
    I make high the low tree;
I dry up the green tree
    And make the dry tree flourish.
I the LORD have spoken;
    I will accomplish it' (17:24)."

The Secret of the Empire

"Sorry," claimed Jameson, "but what were these fresh insights you promised?"

"Well, first of all, I said we *might* get some fresh insights," to which both Sol and Jameson offered a wry smile. "My thought was that discussing politics and religion as a fable was designed to soften the blow. So, my insight was that we need to talk about politics and religion, but we need to learn how to do it with respect."

"I agree," said a smiling Sol. "Relationships are everything. If we can't get along, there must be something wrong with our relationship with God. I remember at our premarital counseling the pastor said that communication is the key to success. And if we communicate with respect, we have a better chance than when it's all about anger and frustration."

"I like that," said Jameson, "and now I would respectfully ask that we go to lunch."

That got three confirming votes so we headed to Sol's choice of Las 3 Abuelas. That means "The Three Grandmothers," and the restaurant was subtitled Cocina Tradicional Mexicana which means "Traditional Mexican Kitchen." It turned out to be a breakfast & brunch place that also handled special events, but we were lucky on both counts. We weren't too late to eat and no special events were happening. Jameson ordered a Combination Plate, Sol tried the Chile Relleno, and I had the Huevos Benedictinosa la Mexicana. As we left, we all agreed that the food was wonderful, but Sol said, "My culture is all about hospitality, and it was disappointing to have such slow service." Returning to our bench at Parque Roma, we settled in with pleasantly full stomachs.

"Next, God refutes negative ideas behind how God governs the moral order, and calls the exilic community to have a stand-up type of character. If a person is righteous, 'he shall surely live, says the Lord GOD' (18:9). If he has a son who practices violence, 'he shall surely die; his blood is upon himself' (18:13)."

"I'm not following," mentioned Sol with a furrowed brow.

"The point is that the popular belief of the day was that God was judge and we had no say in the matter. Ezekiel continues with an example of a grandson. If he sees the error of his father's ways and does not do likewise, 'he shall not die for his father's iniquity; he shall surely live' (18:17). This was a monumental change for God's people because they had fallen so far away from God's ways. Here's the point: 'The person who sins shall die. A child shall not suffer for the iniquity of a parent, nor a parent suffer for the iniquity of a child; the righteousness of the righteous shall be his own, and the wickedness of the wicked shall be his own' (18:20).

"Maybe," said Sol, "this passage was on Jim's mind when his Hole in the Rock Gang saw a man blind from birth. They asked Jim, 'Teacher, who sinned, this man or his parents, that he was born blind?' Jim answered, 'Neither this man nor his parents sinned'" (John 9:2-3)."

"Very nice, Sol, thanks. Here's how the chapter ends. God says, 'Repent and turn from all your transgressions; otherwise iniquity will be your ruin. Cast away from you all the transgressions that you have committed against me, and get yourselves a new heart and a new spirit! Why will you die? For I have no pleasure in the death of anyone, says the Lord GOD. Turn, then, and live' (18:30-32). For what it's worth, that's what I believe. Just like a judge in court doesn't really judge anyone, it's that persons actions that brings judgment upon them. Likewise, when we die and stand before the judge, judgment day becomes about our actions. We need not worry about God being corrupt, just us."

"And just us," suggested Jameson, "is proper justice. I guess we have no one to blame but ourselves."

"That's what God was trying to get his people to understand. They had gone so far astray that they lost their Promised Land."

"Is that the secret of the empire?" asked Jameson.

"A very large part of it, indeed. Now let's hear about the next chapter. It's simply a lament about the politics of power going to the head. The secret of the empire is that Zedekiah lost control of the Promised Land. 'And fire has gone out from its stem, has consumed its branches and fruit, so that there remains in it no strong stem, no scepter for ruling' (19:14).

"Ooh!" proclaimed Jameson. "Now you're offering answers to the secret of the empire."

"That's exactly it. There are many answers and many secrets, and more will be shared later. The story in Ezekiel takes an abrupt change in chapter 20, and some call it a revisionist history. The exilic community needs to understand that Tenochtitlan's judgment was inevitable and a just action from God, and they needed to see God's vision. Ezekiel then retells salvation history with an emphasis on Aztec idolatry. With this new vision of their sinful past, the LORD says: 'As a pleasing odor I will accept you, when I bring you out from the peoples, and gather you out of the countries where you have been scattered; and I will manifest my holiness among you in the sight of the nations' (20:41).

"Next, Ezekiel's attention is drawn to the people remaining in Mexico. The LORD told him to, 'set your face toward Tenochtitlan and preach against the sanctuaries; prophecy against the land of Mexico' and let them know that, 'I am coming against you, and will draw my sword out of its sheath, and will cut off from you both righteous and wicked' (21:1-3). The book continues with a poem about God's sword, interpreted as Cortés coming against Zedekiah. It ends with 'I will pour out my indignation upon you, with the fire of my wrath I will blow upon you. I will deliver you into brutish hands, those skillful to destroy. You shall be fuel for the fire, your blood shall enter the earth; you shall be remembered no more, for I the LORD have spoken' (21:31-32)."

"I was hoping we would be past all those old stories of bloodshed," complained Jameson.

"I liked," said Sol, "that Ezekiel was told by the LORD to 'set your face toward Tenochtitlan.'

"Why do you like that, Mom?"

"Because when Jim Caldwell came down from the Hole in the Rock, he set his face toward Tenochtitlan, and ultimately the noose that took his life."

"Nice connections, hon. I like it, and now for chapter 22. It is about shedding blood and making idols. The point is to show the rapid disintegration of those remaining in Mexico. Chapter 23 is an allegory that shows the deviant behavior of the Mexicans, by talking about them as prostitutes and adulterers. 'She did not give up her whorings that she had practiced since Guatemala...Therefore I delivered her into the hands of her lovers, into the hands of the Spanish Conquistadors' (23:8-9)."

"Can we move on?" requested Sol. "This is pretty intense to have to listen to in the presence of my husband and son."

"We're moving to the unspeakable conclusion of the end of the Holy City, so just hang in there. Chapter 24 begins with the date when Cortés started his siege of Tenochtitlan. It is described in yet another metaphor."

The Secret of the Empire

"Not more prostitutes, I hope," said Jameson.

"No. This time it's the image of a boiling pot."

"What would that signify?" asked Sol.

"Sadly, it's the bloody city, and the Lord GOD says, 'Woe to the bloody city!' (24:9). The story continues with, 'when I cleansed you in your filthy lewdness, you did not become clean from your filth; you shall not again be cleansed until I have satisfied my fury upon you. I the LORD have spoken; the time is coming, I will act. I will not refrain, I will not spare, I will not relent. According to your ways and your doings I will judge you, says the Lord GOD' (24:13-14).

"At this point in Ezekiel's prophecy, things turn personal. The LORD tells him his wife will die and he is not to mourn. 'So I spoke to the people in the morning, and at evening my wife died. And on the next morning I did as I was commanded' (24:18).

"I don't get that at all," said a shocked Sol.

"Neither did the exilic community. They asked, 'Will you not tell us what these things mean for us, that you are acting this way?' (24:19). Ezekiel explained that they needed to lose their understanding of God being present in the temple, and imitate Ezekiel's lack of grief. "And you, mortal, on the day when I take from them their stronghold, their joy and glory, the delight of their eyes and their heart's affection, one who has escaped will come and report to you the news. On that day your mouth shall be opened to the one who has escaped, and you shall speak and no longer be silent. So you shall be a sign to them; and they shall know that I am the LORD' (24:25-27)."

"Surely that means break time for us," suggested Jameson, so we took a silent stroll through the park and thought about the profound secret of the empire. It was a lovely walk through wooded paths with statues and memorials, playgrounds and beautiful views of the mountains. It crossed my mind that it would have been an almost incomprehensible thing to be in captivity and hear about the loss of your homeland. Tears started to well up in my eyes as I thought about the death of Ezekiel's wife and how blessed I was to have Sol by my side. She saw my tears and simply nodded. It was really quite profound that many years together could allow unspoken understandings.

"When we got back to our park bench I mentioned that the next seven chapter were oracles against Mexico's neighbors, then I would follow with a story about the final fall of the Southern Empire."

"Hope the next seven chapters go fast," said a gloomy Sol.

After ignoring that understandable comment I said, "Ezekiel had a pattern for what he wrote next. He prophesied, on the LORD's behalf, about seven nations. The seventh was Guatemala, and it alone got seven oracles. Any idea why Ezekiel used seven?"

"Dad! You act like we don't listen. We know that seven is the number of wholeness, but in what way does that make them whole?"

"It doesn't. Seven can also mean "complete," and I suspect Ezekiel was saying that the LORD's anger toward the nations was whole."

"Maybe," said Jameson, "but doesn't sound very holy."

"Ah, you touch on a touchy subject there. Some biblical scholars suggest seeing the same God in the Old Testament as you notice in the New Testament. Which means that some of the authors might be adding their perspective."

"Move it along," Sol said with indignation.

The Secret of the Empire

"Okay. The first was Belize: 'Because you have clapped your hands and stamped your feet and rejoiced with all the malice within you against the land of Mexico, therefore I have stretched out my hand against you' (25:6-7). Next was Costa Rica and the LORD complained that they didn't find anything special about Mexico. Third was Panama, indicted for being vengeful, then Nicaragua was in trouble for the same reason.

"Fifth up for God's wrath was Honduras, and it was a big one. Chapter 26 brings us ever closer to the end of the Promised Land, because it talks about Cortés and his Spanish Conquistadors being used to fight against Honduras. Chapter 27 offers a lament over Honduras for its pride, while the next chapter offers an oracle against the King of Honduras for his pride. Chapter 28 continues with a lamentation over the King of Honduras, then takes aim at Colombia: 'I will send pestilence into it, and bloodshed into its streets; and the dead shall fall in its midst, by the sword that is against it on every side. And they shall know that I am the LORD' (28:23).

"Before moving into the seven oracles against the seventh nation, Ezekiel shares a word of hope for Mexico from the LORD: 'When I gather the house of Mexico from the peoples among whom they are scattered, and manifest my holiness in them in the sight of the nations, then they shall settle on their own soil that I gave to my servant Tobillo' (28:25).

"Now we're in the final four chapters of Ezekiel, before we look at the fall of the Southern Empire and the devastating destruction of Templo Mayor. In the coming days, we'll discuss the life of the Aztecs in the Exile, followed by the prophets who spoke upon returning home after the Exile. Meanwhile, chapters 29-32 share the seven oracles against the seventh nation: Guatemala.

The Secret of the Empire

1. Chapter 29:1-16. This oracle is against the king's pride for saying, "Lake Izabal is my own; I made it for myself" (vs. 3). God is mad, and continues with judgment against the whole land: "they shall never again be the reliance of the house of Mexico; they will recall their iniquity, when they turned to them for aid. Then they shall know that I am the LORD God" (vs. 16).
2. Chapter 29:17-21. This is an oracle against Guatemala: "I will give the land of Guatemala to Hernando Cortés of Spain; and he shall carry off its wealth and despoil it and plunder it; and it shall be the wages for his army" (vs. 17).
3. Chapter 30:1-19. This is a lamentation of God's judgment against Guatemala: "the day of the LORD is near" (vs. 3), because "its proud might shall come down" (vs.6), so the "most terrible of the nations, shall be brought in to destroy the land" (vs.11). Ezekiel polishes this off with a list of cities that will be in trouble.
4. Chapter 30:20-26. This is a proclamation against the King: "I am against the King of Guatemala, and will break his arms, both the strong arm and the one that was broken; and I will make the sword fall from his hand" (vs.22), then the LORD will "scatter the Guatemalans among the nations and disperse them throughout the countries" (vs. 26).
5. Chapter 31:1-18. In this oracle Ezekiel returns to allegory, using a cosmic tree that is nourished by deep waters (vs. 4). The problem was that "its heart was proud of its height" (vs. 10), so God "closed the

deep over it and covered it" (vs. 15). It closes with a question: "Which among the trees of Eden was like you in glory and in greatness? Now you shall be brought down" (vs. 18).

6. Chapter 32:1-16. This is followed by a lamentation over both the King and Guatemala. It starts with an accusation: "You consider yourself a lion among the nations, but you are like a dragon in the seas" (vs. 2). Verses 3-10 are reminiscent of the Mayan creation myth of Guatemala called the Popol Vuh, while the ending says, "This is a lamentation; it shall be chanted" (vs. 16).

7. Chapter 32:17-32. This final oracle against Guatemala is a dirge about its descent to the Mayan Underworld called Xibalba, which means "The Place of Fright." The LORD said, "wail over the hordes of Guatemala, and send them down to the world below, with those who go down to the Cave" (vs. 18).

"This was the preparation for the Exile. The fall of King Hezekiah and the Southern Empire, to Cortés and the Conquistadors was brutal and final. We'll look at some of the sparse understandings we have in the Aztec Scriptures, then spend some time debriefing our learnings of the day.

"The destruction occurred in two parts: 1) the holy city, Tenochtitlan, and 2) the house of the LORD, Templo Mayor. First of all, it wasn't Montezuma who lost the city to Cortés, as is the popular belief, it was Zedekiah."

Jamesons asked, "So why do people believe these kinds of things?"

The Secret of the Empire

"It's more about it being tradition because Montezuma was the Aztec King that the story surrounds, but it definitely was Zedekiah. Montezuma died before the Empire divided. The final problem began when Zedekiah rebelled against Cortés who 'came with all his army against Tenochtitlan, and laid siege to it; they built siege-works against it all around' (2 Kings 25:1). Being cut off from the world, the residents had no food and a famine set in. Cortés and his army made a breach in the wall, so Zedekiah and his soldiers fled by night. Cortés' army pursued them and overtook them, and Zedekiah's army deserted him. He was brought to Cortés 'who passed sentence on him. They slaughtered the sons of Zedekiah before his eyes, then put out the eyes of Zedekiah; they bound him in fetters and took him to Spain' (2 Kings 25:6-7).

"The next thing they needed to do was destroy the holy city. The captain of Cortés' army came to Tenochtitlan and 'burned down the house of the LORD, the king's house, and all the houses' (2 Kings 25:9). They broke down the walls around the city and 'carried into exile the rest of the people who were left in the city...But the captain of the guard left some of the poorest people of the land to be vinedressers and tillers of the soil' (2 Kings 25:11-12).

"After this they destroyed Templo Mayor. Jeremiah had warned the people that they had broken their relationship with God and would lose their land, but they refused to believe. He prophesied the word of the LORD: 'Amend your ways and your doings, and let me dwell with you in this place. Do not trust in these deceptive words: "This is the temple of the LORD, the temple of the LORD, the temple of the LORD" (Jeremiah 7:3-4). The promise to God's people turned out to make them arrogant, and they paid the price. The conquistadors took the bronze pillars and broke 'them in pieces, and carried the bronze to Spain' (2 Kings 25:13).

"After that, the conquistadors 'took away the pots, the shovels, the snuffers, the dishes for incense, and all the bronze vessels used in the temple service, as well as the firepans and the basins. What was made of gold the captain of the guard took away for the gold, and what was made of silver, for the silver' (2 Kings 25:14-15). In other words, they plundered the holy temple in the holy city, and legend says that the amount of bronze that was taken was beyond weighing. Okay. Let's all take a deep breath, then share what learnings we've had today."

After a long pause, Jameson said, "I hated Nahum. You guys taught me to never gloat when troubles happen to those who don't like us."

"It certainly comes from the teachings of Jim Caldwell, but thanks for the kudos to us."

Sol responded with, "I loved Nahum, because Columbia deserved destruction. They were guilty, and those who remained in Mexico stayed in Sinaloa and formed The Cartel. If ever a group deserved destruction, it is them. They are the complete opposite of our Caldwellian faith."

I waited for a moment, then said, "I'm surprised that I found the book consoling. It reminds me that God can be counted on to destroy enemies of people who trust in God."

"I had terrible troubles with a boss one time," announced Sol, "and I really wanted vengeance. That anger in me never resolved, but I think good old Nahum helped me. God will take care of things in the long run."

"Good to hear, dear."

After giving me a hug, she said, "I liked how Ezekiel

prepared for his ministry, just like Jesus did."

All of a sudden, Jameson had a burst of energy, and said, "I loved the UFO story at the beginning of Ezekiel!"

I frowned and said, "I trust you're joking." Jameson gave an impish smile and shrugged his shoulders, then I said, "I enjoyed how Ezekiel's prophecy came true."

"Please explain that one, Dad"

"Only the prophecies that came true were the ones that made it into the Bible. It makes me wonder what the prophecies that didn't make it were all about."

Sol then volunteered, "I found it interesting that Ezekiel was lifted by the spirit to see his homeland, and then returned spiritually to the exiles. I had an out-of-body experience when I was a child. I received terrible burns on my legs and was in the hospital for a long time. Early on I heard the doctors say that I wouldn't make it, and my spirit was lifted up so that I was able to look down on the scene. I found myself sitting on a shelf next to a doll and the doll said, 'The doctors don't know what they are talking about. You're going to make it.'"

"Wow! What a great story. I mean, sorry that happened to you, but I guess it feels pretty good to be alive and to tell the story."

"Yes it does, son, because now I have you and your father in my life."

We all got choked up a bit, then Jameson asked me, "Didn't you say something about hope?"

"Yes. What the exiled community learned was that hope is in God, not themselves."

Next, Sol said, "I could have done without the last half of what we heard today. Oracles, and allegories, and visions, and metaphors, and laments probably have their place, but I prefer the Good News of Jim Caldwell."

"Just remember that it's all 'God's Word.' What I love about that thought is, knowing the authors offered their perspective, means it's not all 'God's words.' Now let's pack up, head for the car, be thankful for a beautiful day in Parque Roma, get a nice dinner and a good night's rest. Tomorrow we will hear about the experience in exile."

ACT III
During the Exile

The Secret of the Empire

SCENE ONE
Ezekiel 33-58

It was a gorgeous day outside, but Sol and Jameson knew I was up to something.

"Okay," announced Sol, who probably knew me better than I knew myself. "What's going on?"

"What?" I asked sheepishly.

"Come on, Dad. You should never gamble because you can't hide excitement."

"Okay, I admit it. Something pretty cool is going to happen."

"What is it?" asked Sol, who can't ever wait for surprises.

"Nope. Not this time. Let's just go downstairs and get in the car."

"But we haven't had breakfast yet!" complained Jameson.

"Ah, the glint in your father's eyes tells me it has something to do with breakfast, but I can't imagine that being so exciting."

We finally headed downstairs from our hotel room and got in the car. I plugged my phone in to the map and entered an address, and off we went.

Jameson was in the passenger seat and was desperately trying to figure out the mystery when he asked, "Does this have anything to do with the secret of the empire?"

I just laughed and left them in the void of unknowing. Sol was enjoying being in Mexico, so she spontaneously broke into one of her favorite songs, La Bikina, by Luis Miguel. Soon we were in the suburb of Santa Catarina, then headed northwest to the city Garcia. From there we headed out of town to the northeast and my fellow passengers started getting pretty frustrated. When we passed a sign that said Xenpal, Jameson looked it up and said, "We're going to a zoo?" We drove right past and both of them were now getting exasperated.

Next we went past a campground and Sol sarcastically said, "I hope you haven't taken us out here for breakfast!"

The scenery was fantastic, with craggy mountain crests constantly getting closer, but we continued on. At this point the road came to an end with a loop for the return trip.

"You're lost, aren't you!" demanded Sol.

I then turned on to a singular road that went back to an old farmhouse, and Jameson said, "Kinda' creepy, Dad. Did you ever read *In Cold Blood*?"

It was an old farmhouse on a large expanse of land with lots of farming equipment, and I opened my door and got out. It took a bit of coaxing to get them to cooperate, but soon enough I was knocking on the front door. When it creaked open, a rather scary looking, short and stocky Mexican man with a long beard was standing there with his leg bent on a knee scooter.

Jameson nearly screamed, "Geraldo!" who almost tipped over when Jameson ran up to give him a hug.

After lots of laughter, I finally introduced him to Sol who was quite astonished at the developments. "Geraldo was our tour guide last year."

After I introduced Sol, Geraldo's wife came to greet us all and said, "I have the best breakfast you'll ever have. It's all ready to go. My name is Rivera."

Jameson couldn't miss the chance to say, "So together you are Geraldo Rivera?"

Geraldo tried to act hurt for a moment but couldn't keep the laughter at bay. Then Rivera said, "Actually my parents were big fans of Frida Kahlo, but they didn't like either of her names, so they chose her husband's last name of Rivera."

The Secret of the Empire

We had much to talk about, so Rivera suggested we continue the conversation over breakfast. We happily took a seat at their kitchen table with its sumptuous spread of homemade tortillas made fresh on a placa, huevos rancheros, and an amazing bean skillet like I had never seen. To the side was an array of homemade jams and jellies and salsas, and by each plate was a glass of atole. Geraldo offered grace and Rivera began passing the food around.

"Okay, Dad, so how did you know Geraldo lived here?"

"Remember sitting at the Great Pyramid of Cholula?

"How could I forget?" Jameson said with a huge smile.

"That's where Geraldo told us about the Aztec people getting organized into twelve tribes."

"Okay."

"And you got excited about the most well-known cities currently in each tribal area, like Puerto Vallarta, Acapulco, and Oaxaca."

"I hope you're going somewhere with this."

"Then Geraldo asked if we knew what Monterrey was well-known for."

"Vaguely familiar, but what was the answer?"

Geraldo then beamed as he reminded, "Because it is where I was born!"

All five of us laughed heartily for a while, then Jameson asked, "So how did you know he lived here?"

I pointed at the knee scooter next to Geraldo and asked, "Remember when I said Geraldo couldn't be our guide this time because he had a farming accident?" Jameson and Sol both acknowledged, then I said, "We've kept in touch."

The conversation continued while eating great food, and when we were done Sol offered to help Rivera clean up so "the boys" could finish their conversation. It was certainly a visit to remember and we hated to go, but before long my agenda orientation took over. We said our fond farewells then I said "adios" as we got in the car. Geraldo said "adios" back to us and Jameson seemed a bit confused, so Sol explained as we went down the driveway, "it simply means 'go with God.' It's a great word for hello and goodbye, just like the Hawaiian word 'aloha.'"

As we drove down the long driveway, Jameson said, "That was the best! Thanks, Dad." Even Sol said it was a great idea and she was glad it worked out. Soon we made our way to Parque Fundidora, got out of the car, and found some benches facing the Rio Santa Catarina.

Another wonderful day of sunshine and shade awaited us as we settled in for a day of learning. A gentle breeze rose from the river and refreshed us as I began. "Ezekiel's story continued with a discussion of how God would hold him accountable to warn the wicked ones. 'But if you warn the wicked to turn from their ways, and they do not turn from their ways, the wicked shall die in their iniquities, but you will have saved your life' (33:9).

"The problem was that the demoralized exiles were concerned for their own lives. God told Ezekiel to tell them, 'I have no pleasure in the death of the wicked, but that the wicked turn from their ways and live; turn back, turn back from your evil ways; for why will you die, O house of Mexico?' (33:11)."

Jameson said, "Not sensing much comfort."

"Then listen to what God had to say next: 'None of the sins that they have committed shall be remembered against them; they have done what is lawful and right, they shall surely live' (33:16). This was to prepare the exilic community for the fall of the Southern Empire, where someone who had escaped from

The Secret of the Empire

Tenochtitlan came to Ezekiel and said, 'The city has fallen.' This must have come as a crushing blow. They lost their Promised Land because they quit following God's commandments, but if they returned to being God's People by following the commandments, they could hope to get back their Promised Land. I'm a very visual person, so let me draw this:

"Not bad," said Jameson with a chuckle, "but let's just say drawing isn't your strong point."

"Actually, I like it," offered Sol. "If God's People move back to following the Commandments, they could regain the Promised Land."

"Great! Maybe that college class I took on geometry paid off!" Both of them looked confused, so I moved on. "In the next chapter Ezekiel says the first step in the right direction is to understand that the leadership back in Mexico was corrupt. God chose to use the image of sheep and shepherd, but it wasn't about having the leaders become better shepherds. 'For thus says the Lord GOD: I myself will search for my sheep, and will seek them out' (34:11)."

"Yep," agreed Sol. "Jim was willing to do anything to find the one lost sheep."

"And that was a parable, where Jim Caldwell probably got inspiration from this chapter, and Jim also called himself the good shepherd in John 10:11."

Sol spoke up again and said, "Don't forget Montezuma saying that 'The LORD is my shepherd,' in Psalm 23:1."

"Wait," complained Jameson, "this is getting rather dizzying, so what's the point?"

"Try this," I offered. "God says, 'I will seek the lost, and I will bring back the strayed, and I will bind up the injured, and I will strengthen the weak, but the fat and the strong I will destroy. I will feed them with justice' (34:16). To me this emphasizes that we need to turn to God, then, now, and always."

"Amen!" exclaimed an almost jubilant Sol with both arms raised in the air.

"From here it gets a bit strange, because the LORD pronounces an oracle against Panama in chapter 35."

"I'll pass," frowned Jameson.

"Me, too. After all, we're people of the Good News. Which is where chapter 36 turns. After the LORD spends some more time denouncing Panama, we hear, 'But you, O mountains of Mexico, shall shoot out your branches, and yield your fruit to my people Mexico; for they shall soon come home' (36:8). Rather than being against his people, God is planning to be on their side. 'I will multiply human beings and animals upon you. They shall increase and be fruitful; and I will cause you to be inhabited as in your former times, and will do more good to you than ever before. Then you shall know that I am the LORD' (36:11).

"The Lord God continues offering this vision to Ezekiel to prophesy to the people: 'On the day that I cleanse you from all your iniquities, I will cause the towns to be inhabited, and the waste places shall be rebuilt...And they will say, "This land that was desolate has become like the garden of Aztlan"' (36:33, 35)."

"Been there, done that!" claimed a smiling Jameson.

"What do you mean?" asked Sol.

"That's where dad and I started last year's adventure, sitting at the Tikal Temple in the jungles of Guatemala," as Sol looked on approvingly.

"Next comes one of the more memorable chapters in Ezekiel, known as *The Valley of Dry Bones*. To do it justice, let me just read the vision offered in the first six verses:

> The hand of the LORD came upon me, and he brought me out by the spirit of the LORD and set me down in the middle of a valley; it was full of bones. He led me all around them; there were very many lying in the valley, and they were very dry. He said to me, "Mortal, can these bones live?" I answered, "O Lord GOD, you know." Then he said to me, "Prophesy to these bones, and say to them: O dry bones, hear the word of the LORD. Thus says the Lord GOD to these bones: I will cause breath to enter you, and you shall live. I will lay sinews on you, and will cause flesh to come upon you, and cover you with skin, and put breath in you, and you shall live; and you shall know that I am the LORD."

The Secret of the Empire

"I know what happened next!" said a captivated Jameson. "The bones came together, and the renewed people stood on their feet. It's a great vision of hope for people who are down and out."

"Very good, son. Very good. The rest of chapter 37 uses the image of two sticks to represent the Northern Empire and the Southern Empire. God tells Ezekiel to 'join them together into one stick' (vs. 17), signifying their ultimate unification. God finishes this story with, 'Then the nations shall know that I the LORD sanctify Mexico, when my sanctuary is among them forever' (vs. 28). Next the story takes a strange turn to 'Gog, of the land of Magog' (38:2)."

"I know all about that!" said Sol with a huge frown. "That's from the Book of Revelation."

"You got that right," I cautioned, "because the Revelation story was adapted from these two chapters. It was a vision about feeling secure once they return to the Promised Land. The point was that nobody can thwart God's ultimate plans. The word from God was 'I will turn you around and put hooks into your jaws, and I will lead you out with all your army' (38:4). The LORD continues with, 'and I will not let my holy name be profaned any more; and the nations shall know that I am the LORD, the Holy One of Mexico. It has come! It has happened, says the Lord GOD. This is the day of which I have spoken' (39:7-8). Here comes another seven, concerning the burial of Gog. 'Seven months the house of Mexico shall spend burying them, in order to cleanse the land' (39:12)."

"Oh, I get it," announced Jameson. "The death of God's enemies means a complete cleansing of the land."

"And for the apocalypse!" proclaimed Sol.

"Sounds like a good time to take a lunch break." They both

The Secret of the Empire

agreed and Sol mentioned that she saw a nearby store where she would like to shop, then Jameson said that he would like to find a baseball cap with the word Monterrey on it. We agreed to take thirty minutes and meet back at the El Lingote restaurant. When we regathered, we found out that they didn't open until one, so we had thirty more minutes to kill. We then agreed to take a stroll around the park. Jameson checked the map on his phone and said there was a short round trip on the walkways. We paused for a moment at Canal Santa Lucia, then headed north past Casa Rosa. The weather was beginning to warm up, so we took the next path to the right and stopped at Conarte, an Arts pavilion. After a brief visit, we headed back south and the path took us straight to El Lingote just as they opened.

"Hey, Dad. I saw some great seats with views if we sit out on the terrace."

"Okay, I'll check." It turned out to be a much fancier restaurant than I expected, but since we were there right at opening time, we got our choice of seats. The terrace was amazing with beautiful views of the mountains in the distance, but it turned out that the service and food was even better. We were treated exceptionally well, and I wondered if having Sol speak Spanish to the server was part of the reason. Let me just say that I ordered Pulpo Norestense, and here is how it was described in the menu: Pulpo a la parrilla en adobo de chiles secos, con risotto de asado de Puerco, chicahrron de pork belly, garbanzo y salsa macha.

Sol laughed when I tried to pronounce it, but at least I could understand about half of what was in it. Far more importantly, it had a heavenly fragrance and out-of-this-world flavor. I don't even know what Sol and Jameson ordered because I was too entranced by my gastronomic experience. We all three enjoyed a classic margarita, but Sol struggled a bit with the idea that her son was growing up. After lunch, we decided to relax a bit to let the meal settle, then slowly made our way back to the bench by the river to hear the final nine chapters of Ezekiel.

"Chapters 40-48 envision a new social order of God's people again living on their God-promised land. God will be the new king and the Temple will need to be restored. They will need to relearn how to live with the divine presence, and the land will need to be rid of violence and injustice. To accomplish this, the first thing God does is transport Ezekiel to the land of Mexico and sets him down on a mountain. Again he has an experience with a Jacob Marley type of guide who tells him to 'look closely and attentively' (40:4). The purpose of this visit was to encourage fellow exiles to believe that they will become the house of Mexico. The guide went about doing lots of measuring, but I'll spare you the details."

"Thanks, Dad!" Even Sol looked relieved.

"In the big picture, the guide measured the exterior of the temple, then did the same for the interior. After that, the guide showed the sanctuary and the altar and the inner court, in his tour for Ezekiel. Finally the guide spoke again, saying, 'The north chambers and the south chambers opposite the vacant area are the holy chambers' (42:13). But here's the important thing. The guide took Ezekiel to the gate, and there, 'the glory of the God of Mexico was coming from the east' (43:2)."

"Obviously," said Jameson, "this is important, but specifically, why?"

"It's because it is a vision of the reversal of the LORD's departure from the temple and the city. The departure was frightening enough, so the exilic community needed this vision to give them hope. Then a voice came from the temple and said, 'this is the place of my throne and the place for the soles of my feet, where I will reside among the people of Mexico forever' (43:7). The voice then told Ezekiel to tell his people the plan of the temple, and said, 'This is the law of the temple: the whole territory on the top of the mountain all around shall be most holy. This is the law of the temple' (43:12).

"What comes next is a reordering of life toward holiness, purity, justice, and economic equity. It begins with seven days of consecration of the altar."

"Wait a minute," requested Jameson. "Is the exile over?"

"No, but the practical applications sure sound that way, don't they?" Jameson looked mildly embarrassed, so I assured him it was a good question. "Here's what was said next: 'When these days are over, then from the eighth day onward the priests shall offer upon the altar your burnt offerings and your offerings of well-being; and I will accept you, says the Lord GOD' (43:27).

Sol seemed intent on helping to alleviate Jameson's embarrassment, so she said, "Sure sounds to me like everyone is back in Mexico."

Jameson smiled and said, "I'm alright, mom. Thanks."

"Next, the LORD said to Ezekiel, 'This gate shall remain shut; it shall not be opened, and no one shall enter by it; for the LORD, the God of Mexico, has entered by it; therefore it shall remain shut' (44:2).

"And the purpose of that?" asked Jameson.

"I think it means that the LORD will never again depart from the Temple. God then told Ezekiel that the Levites who had gone astray would serve a purpose. 'I will appoint them to keep charge of the temple, to do all its chores, all that is to be done in it' (44:14)."

"Ooh," said Jameson. "A bit of vengeance. Cool."

"But the Levitical priests who stayed faithful while Mexico went astray would be assigned to minster to God."

"How would they do that?" inquired Jameson.

"By not shaving their head, nor drinking wine when they enter the inner court. They are also not to 'marry a widow, or a divorced woman, but only a virgin of the stock of the house of Mexico, or a widow who is the widow of a priest' (44:22)"

"I hope you are listening, Jameson," exclaimed Sol in an almost scolding voice.

"Mom!"

Quickly getting back to the task at hand, I said that they were to teach, act as judges as needed, and follow proper procedures toward the dead. The attention then turned to the area outside the temple. A portion was to be set aside as a holy district, followed by an area for the city. Then Ezekiel is told to have them observe honesty in weights and measures, and make offerings so that the LORD would also not be defrauded. Next was a discussion of festivals, concentrating on the reestablishment of Passover.

"Chapter 46 talks about the Sabbath and some miscellaneous regulations, then chapter 47 shows the effects of having the divine presence in the land. 'Then he brought me back to the entrance of the temple' there, water was flowing from below the threshold of the temple toward the east (for the temple faced east); and the water was flowing down from below the south end of the threshold of the temple, south of the altar. Then he brough me out by way of the north gate, and led me around on the outside to the outer gate that faces toward the east; and the water was coming out on the south side' (47:1-2).'"

The Secret of the Empire

"Sorry," said Jameson. "What is that all about?"

"It's to set up contrast. The next several verses talk about the guide leading Ezekiel through the water. At first it is ankle-deep, then knee-deep, then waist-deep, then deep enough to swim."

"So?" asked a mildly perturbed Jameson.

"It is to show the beauty of God's presence, and here's how. 'On the banks, on both sides of the river, there will grow all kinds of trees for food. Their leaves will not wither no their fruit fail, but they will bear fresh fruit every month, because the water for them flows from the sanctuary. Their fruit will be for food, and their leaves for healing' (47:12). After that the land was equitably divided among the twelve tribes. The Lord GOD said, 'you shall divide this land among you according to the tribes of Mexico' (47:21). The city itself does not belong to any particular tribe, so it is renamed: 'And the name of the city from that time on shall be, The LORD is There' (48:35), which later became Mexico City.

"That ends the book of the prophet Ezekiel. Time to share your learnings."

"Not so much a learning," said a thoughtful Jameson, "but I have a question."

"Of course!"

Jameson thought for a moment to formulate his question, then asked, "Why does God seem to be evil sometimes?"

Sol looked shocked, and turned to her body language of folded arms, then I said, "I thought that question might come up. I did some research this past year, and found that what you're talking about is sometimes referred to as divine justice, but then it gets a bit trickier." All of a sudden Sol perked up with obvious intrigue, and I continued. "You have to start with the idea of justice. Now wait a minute, I want to check a note on my phone to give you the correct quotation." After a brief pause, I said, "Okay, here it is: 'Justice is a philosophical concept of rightness in ethics and is part of the central core of morality.'"

Sol threw her hands in the air and said, "Sounds like what some haughty professor would say!"

"I don't disagree. It needs to be more practical to be useful. Try this. Some scholars say that justice is whatever God says it is."

"That's more like it!" beamed Sol. "God is sovereign!"

"All I know is that the Bible oftentimes says the righteous will be rewarded and the wicked will be punished."

"Tell us more about that, Dad."

After thumbing through my phone, I found several characteristic verses. "Remember when Geraldo was talking about Sodom and Gomorrah?" Jameson nodded, then I continued. "It is a classic story of crime and punishment, and says, 'keep the way of the LORD by doing righteousness and justice' (Genesis 18:19).

"What about the punishment part?" asked a mildly frustrated Sol.

"Well, here's a setup story from the book of Judges. 'It is not I who have sinned against you, but you are the one who does me wrong, by making war on me. Let the LORD, who is judge, decide today' (11:27)."

"Ready for the knockout punch," said a now exasperated Sol.

"Okay, here it is. My point is that concentrating on bad news might cause us to miss out on the good news." Sol again folded her arms, then I went on. "We recently dealt with the book of Amos, where with the famous quote, 'But let justice roll down like waters, and righteousness like an ever-flowing stream' (5:24)."

Jameson then said, "So maybe our task is to let God do the justice part, and let us do the righteousness part."

"Didn't hear a knockout punch," complained Sol.

"Okay, so try this. I already highlighted it a few days ago when we were talking about Micah, but it is certainly worth repeating. 'He has told you, O mortal, what is good; and what does the LORD require of you but to do justice, and to love kindness, and to walk humbly with your God?' (6:8).

"That's great Dad, but it still doesn't explain why God was so mean to the chosen ones."

"Well, that's easy. They quit following God's ways. God's commandments. God's promises. Now, can we get back to your learnings?"

Jameson spoke up first and said, "I love Dickens' *A Christmas Carol*, so I found it pretty neat that the guy who led Ezekiel around the vision of a newly restored Tenochtitlan was like the Jacob Marley character."

"Yes," agreed Sol, "and I loved the part of the prophecy, right after that, when God returned to the Temple."

"I make no bones about it, that one of my favorite stories is the Valley of Dry Bones."

"It's kinda sad, Dad, how you can't keep away from dad jokes."

"To each their own," I said with a big smile. Next, Jameson said that he enjoyed learning where Geraldo lived. "Not exactly a learning about the Bible, but, yes, it was great."

Next, Sol volunteered that she hated that business about Gog. "The Book of Revelation scares me enough that I don't need some Old Testament prophet reminding me of the end times."

"Okay. That's just not it at all. Gog exemplifies the forces of violent domination, and that they will be destroyed. Even in that story we find good news, for those who are looking for it." I quickly turned in my Bible to Ezekiel 37 and read, 'I will make a covenant of peace with them; it shall be an everlasting covenant with them; and I will bless them and multiply them, and will set my sanctuary among them forevermore. My dwelling place shall be with them; and I will be their God, and they shall be my people. Then the nations shall know that I the LORD sanctify Mexico, when my sanctuary is among them forevermore' (vv. 26-28).

"A bit heavy for me," announced Jameson, "so let me say that I loved the restaurant."

I had a huge smile and agreed. "I have no idea what you two had, but my meal was spectacular."

"We know you were oblivious," said Sol. "The food was dripping out of both sides of your mouth."

After some uncomfortable laughter, I said, "I loved that the city of Tenochtitlan was renamed, 'The LORD is there.'"

"Why?" inquired Jameson.

"Because it makes me think that when I was renewed in God's grace, I was renamed a 'Caldwellian.'"

That drew smiles from both of them, then Sol asked, "What did Ezekiel say about turning your life around?"

"Let me look it up." I somehow found it intriguing that I was turning the pages to find about turning life around, but I wasn't about to mention it. "Here it is. 'Now you, mortal, say to the house of Mexico, Thus you have said: "Our transgressions and our sins weigh upon us, and we waste away because of them; how then can we live?" Say to them, As I live, says the Lord

The Secret of the Empire

GOD, I have no pleasure in the death of the wicked, but that the wicked turn from their ways and live; turn back, turn back from your evil ways; for why will you die, O house of Mexico?'"

"Aren't we right back to that righteousness and justice stuff? asked Jameson.

"Well, yes. Didn't I say it was pervasive? But try these verses: 'If the wicked restore the pledge, give back what they have taken by robbery, and walk in the statutes of life, committing no iniquity—they shall surely live, they shall not die. None of the sins that they have committed shall be remembered against them; they have done what is lawful and right, they shall surely live' (Ezekiel 33:15-16)."

"Okay," announced Sol, "I'm ready to move on. I really did like the drawing you did today, about God's People moving back to following the Commandments, and then they could regain the Promised Land. Mexico is too precious to lose for any reason."

Taking an opportunity to balance the compliments, Jameson said, "I learned that the last nine chapters of Ezekiel are amazingly boring."

"Good one, son," I said with a smirk. "Ending on a positive note, let me lift up these verses: 'But you, O mountains of Mexico, shall shoot out your branches, and yield your fruit to my people Mexico; for they shall soon come home. See now, I am for you; I will turn to you, and you shall be tilled and sown; and I will multiply your population, the whole house of Mexico, all of it; the towns shall be inhabited and the waste places rebuilt; and I will multiply human beings and animals upon you. They shall increase and be fruitful; and I will cause you to be inhabited as in your former times, and will do more good to you than ever before. Then you shall know that I am the LORD' (Ezekiel 36:8-11).

The Secret of the Empire

"It's been a great day. Thanks for your attentiveness and interest. We're done a little early, so let's celebrate with a bit of exploring Monterrey." We headed back to the car and drove for a long time, enjoying the culture and creativity of this marvelous city. The one stop we made was to take in an up-close view of the Palacio del Obispado, a Baroque palace that housed a regional museum.

Soon Jameson was on his phone looking for a place to eat. "The hotel is terrific, but I'd to take in more of the local color." We all agreed so he kept looking. "How about seafood?" Again Sol and I were favorable so in very short order he said, "Let's try El Camaron."

When we got there, the place was filled with music. A mariachi band was playing, then a soloist and a guitar player took over. During break time, a server stepped up to the microphone and announced that they would have an open mic time next. I looked at Sol and said, "You've got to do this!"

She smiled and said, "I think I will. There's nothing better than being a Mexican in Mexico singing a Mexican song."

Waiting for the music break to be over, we ordered an appetizer of scalloped octopus and a large shrimp cocktail. As we waited for our dinner, I mentioned that tomorrow we will hear about Isaiah 40-55. Not only is it more of the brief information we have about the exile, but it also is one of my favorite sections of the Bible.

Pretty soon the waiter returned to the microphone and said, "Okay, who wants to come up and sing?"

Sol immediately stood up and made her way to the front. Jameson and I were grinning and applauding because we were so happy for her to get this opportunity. She has a wonderful voice, but only sings special music from time to time at church.

"Gracias," she said to the waiter, then turned to the dining audience. They were mostly eating, but she went ahead and said, "I'd like to sing a favorite song of my mother's called Estrella." Several people looked up as she began singing, and it was almost magical. Not only was she doing a wonderful job, but many in the restaurant joined in. The colorful restaurant, fabulous food, and great music made for a memorable evening. All of a sudden, Jameson became more interested in his Hispanic roots.

SCENE TWO
Isaiah 40-55

    We were blessed this morning with a refreshing rain, which left the birds chirping and an occasional rooster crowing. Jameson requested Parque San Nicolas for our talk, so we drove northwest from our hotel and quickly found a park bench near the Museo de San Nicolas. We brought some towels from the hotel, dried the bench off, and I was pretty excited to get started.

    "One reason I love this book, sometimes called Second Isaiah or Deutero-Isaiah, is because this prophet wasn't about gloom and doom. Isaiah was all about liberation, restoration and salvation."

    "What makes you think Isaiah wasn't written by one prophet?" asked Sol.

    "Thanks. Questioning is always a good thing. One reason scholars today believe Isaiah 40-55 was written 200 years after Isaiah 1-39, is the way chapter 40 begins. 'Comfort, O comfort my people, says your God. Speak tenderly to Tenochtitlan, and cry to her that she has served her term, that her penalty is paid, that she has received from the LORD'S hand double for all her sins' (vv. 1-2)."

    "Sorry," exclaimed Jameson, "but I don't get it."

    "First Isaiah began his prophetic work before the Northern Empire fell to The Cartel, and well before the Southern Empire fell to the Conquistadors. So what's the business about Tenochtitlan's penalty being paid? It makes sense if you let Second Isaiah be written during the exile."

    "Still not there," informed Sol.

    "Let me try better. Later, the LORD says of Cyrus, 'He is

my shepherd, and he shall carry out my purpose'; and says of Tenochtitlan, 'It shall be rebuilt,' and of the temple, 'Your foundation shall be laid' (44:28)."

"I get it," announced Jameson. "Cyrus wasn't even around during First Isaiah, and the temple wasn't destroyed."

"Great! Next I want to mention that Isaiah 40-48 is about promising liberation to the exiles in Spain, and Isaiah 49-55 anticipates the restoration of Tenochtitlan back in Mexico. The first eleven verses of chapter 40 record the commissioning of Second Isaiah. Try to imagine the task he had to bring good news to these beleaguered people. Their world collapsed when the Conquistadors defeated them, destroyed the temple, and exiled them to Spain. For nearly 50 years this group of Aztecs lived in defeat. Their hope was waning, and they were dying in a foreign land.

"Then along comes Isaiah. He sensed that God was ready to do great things again for the Aztec people, so he used imagery from the Exodus. To inspire them, Isaiah's message was going to be filled with joy, so he begins like a general getting stationary troops ready to move. Encouragement comes from a voice crying out from the heavens:

'On the ocean prepare the way of the LORD,
        make straight a shipping lane for our God.
Every valley of water shall be lifted up,
        and every swell shall be made low;
the uneven water shall become level,
        and the rough places made smooth.
Then the glory of the LORD shall be revealed,
        and all people shall see it together,
for the mouth of the LORD has spoken' (40:3-5).

The Secret of the Empire

"I remember glory," said Sol.

"What do you mean?" asked Jameson.

Sol quickly opened her Bible and read, "'Like the bow in a cloud on a rainy day, such was the appearance of the splendor all around. This was the appearance of the likeness of the glory of the LORD.' That's from Ezekiel 1:28, saying that we can see the glory of the LORD, so Isaiah was prophesying that the presence of God would be so strong it would be visible."

Jameson and I looked at each other a bit stunned, then I smiled, thanked her for a great observation, and continued. "Another voice cries out from the heavens and tells Isaiah to preach. After he expresses despair at his challenging task, he digs deep and comes up with the essence of what he has to say to his fellow exiles. 'The grass withers, the flower fades; but the word of our God will stand forever' (40:8)."

"Amen," said a smiling Sol.

"I like it," said Jameson, "especially that verse eight is a one sentence sermon, but just exactly how does that help them?"

"Because it instills the hope they needed that the Promised Land would again be theirs. Even though God's promise seemed to be gone for now, its eternal nature would shine through. The final inspiration Isaiah received was to imagine the exiles returning and give them the good news that God intends to deliver them: 'He will feed his flock like a shepherd; he will gather the lambs in his arms, and carry them in his bosom, and gently lead the mother sheep' (40:11).

"The next section is a hymn that celebrates God as the almighty creator by asking a series of rhetorical questions. The point is that even the captors in Spain are little more than dust. Isaiah increases his boldness by referring to the sun, the moon, and the stars as meaningless in God's much larger universe.

The Secret of the Empire

This is so bold because Spain worshipped them as gods. Can you imagine proclaiming God's superiority while you are still in Spain?"

"Pretty cool," proclaimed Jameson.

"Then Isaiah really gets down to business with the intention of removing the stumbling block of hopelessness. Here's how he puts it:

'Why do you say, "My way is hidden from the LORD,
    and my right is disregarded by my God?"
Have you not known? Have you not heard?
    The LORD is the everlasting God,
the Creator of the ends of the earth.
    He does not faint or grow weary;
his understanding is unsearchable.
    He gives power to the faint,
and strengthens the powerless.
    Even youths will faint and be weary,
and the young will fall exhausted;
    but those who wait for the LORD
shall renew their strength,
    they shall mount up with wings like eagles,
they shall run and not be weary,
    they shall walk and not faint' (40:27-31)."

"Now that's one of my favorite Aztec scripture passages," announced Sol.

I agreed, then said, "Isaiah was trying to help his people see that God was getting ready to create a new thing."

Jameson said, "I can't imagine a tougher task."

I responded that "If you go into the ministry, you just might have the same job trying to incite a struggling church to move forward, or even to move at all."

"Thanks, Dad. Nothing like throwing a wet blanket on a potential calling."

"Sorry. Just trying to toss out a little reality, kind of like what Isaiah was doing next. He offers an oracle of judgment against the nations that brought down Mexico, and a promise of restoration. 'Who has roused a victor from the east, summoned him to his service?' (41:2). Any idea who this victor from the east was?" They looked at me with blank stares, so I said, "It was Cyrus II of Persia who conquered Spain and allowed the exiled Aztecs to return home.

"It was here that God inspired Isaiah to give his people assurance. 'You whom I took from the ends of the earth, and called from its farthest corners, saying to you, "You are my servant, I have chosen you and not cast you off"; do not fear, for I am with you, do not be afraid, for I am your God; I will strengthen you, I will help you, I will uphold you with my victorious right hand' (41:9-10). This is even more impactful in the midst of God's judgment against the other nations."

Jameson said, "I would imagine God would need to offer a lot of hope after the exiled Aztecs experienced generations of hopelessness in a foreign land."

"Sure! That's why he gives an exodus-like vision for their journey back to Mexico. The point of God's upcoming miraculous deeds was 'so that all may see and know, all may consider and understand, that the LORD has done this, the Holy One of Mexico has created it' (41:20). The point was to remember the past and let it become a guide to the future. Even the word 'create' was intentionally used because it is the same word found in the creation story. The idea was that God was getting ready to create a new thing: God's people once again living on the Promised Land. That brings us to what is known as The First Servant Song, where God is speaking about the Aztecs.

> 'Here is my servant, whom I uphold,
>   my chosen, in whom my soul delights;
> I have put my spirit upon him;
>   he will bring forth justice to the nations.
> He will not cry or lift up his voice,
>   or make it heard in the street;
> a bruised reed he will not break,
>   and a dimly burning wick he will not quench;
> he will faithfully bring forth justice.
>   He will not grow faint or be crushed
> until he has established justice in the earth;
>   and the coastlands wait for his teaching (42:1-4).'

"I think I get it," proclaimed Jameson. "To inspire them toward a vision, they needed purpose."

"Proud of you," said Sol, as she patted him on the face.

"To continue the inspiration, Isaiah shares his unique prophecy of good news. 'See, the former things have come to pass, and new things I now declare; before they spring forth, I tell you of them' (42:9). The reason is because they were nearly immune to the new song of hope and deliverance. All they could think about was their punishment in exile, so they desperately needed a powerful vision. 'But now thus says the LORD, he who created you, O Southern Empire, he who formed you, O Northern Empire: Do not fear, for I have redeemed you; I have called you by name, you are mine' (43:1).

The Secret of the Empire

"I just love how specific God is in giving them hope of deliverance and restoration. 'I will say to the north, "Give them up," and to the south, "Do not withhold; bring my sons from far away and my daughters from the end of the earth"' (43:6). What a great way to speak to the community about their context. Not only were they far away, but God is inspiring them that the land itself is calling them back."

"I can relate," said Sol. "Just being here in Monterrey is speaking peace to my soul. Being among God's people on God's promised land is indescribably wonderful, and I am sure that the older ones among the exiles remembered the home land, too."

"Come to think of it, I can relate too. When we took a trip to England, I felt like I was home. It really was almost like the land calling me back. Anyway, Isaiah then gave them some hope that their enemies would be judged."

"Good news for me, and bad news for them, is an interesting balance," said Jameson.

"But it was part of what they needed to hear. Bringing the message home to the exiles, Isaiah offered God's word in this manner: 'I, I am He who blots out your transgressions for my own sake, and I will not remember your sins' (43:25)."

"I get that," said Sol. "Rather than focus on the sins of others, focus on your own sin. And what a beautiful reason to forgive."

"What do you mean, Mom?"

"God needed to forgive for his own sake. Holding on to anger and grudges only poisons the holder, not to mention that God forgets our sins when we ask for forgiveness."

Jameson added, "Happy for God, but I agree with the old thought that, 'I can forgive, but I can never forget.'"

The Secret of the Empire

"An old trick I learned before I met your mother was that things are more memorable when they are important to us. When a bad thing happens, don't focus on it. That makes it somewhat easier to forget."

"Thanks, Dad. I'll have to think about that one, which, I guess would make it more memorable," Jameson said with a slight grin.

"Meanwhile, the prophecy continues the task of getting the exiles to believe their toubled time was over. 'I will pour my spirit upon your descendants, and my blessing on your offspring' (44:3).

"How does that help?" asked Jameson.

"Because it continues the image of everything getting back to normal. The promises will continue after this short break. Well, of course, it was a long break for the exiles. Then Isaiah continues with hope: 'you will not be forgotten by me. I have swept away your transgressions like a cloud, and your sins like mist; return to me, for I have redeemed you' (44:21-22). The prophecy then turns to Cyrus, who is the one coming to bring them their freedom, even though Cyrus did not know God. To show God's superiority over the gods of Spain, the prophecy says, 'I form light and create darkness, I make weal and create woe; I the LORD do all these things' (45:7)."

"So God creates evil?" asked Jameson.

"It's what the scriptures say here. Think back for a moment to our discussion of theodicy. Otherwise, focus on the good news. Focus on hope. The exiles needed to know that God punished them, which is darkness, but now they are forgiven, which is light. Isaiah then talks about how understandable it is to not be able to understand God: 'Truly, you are a God who hides himself' (45:15). He continues with a condemnation of the gods of Spain."

"Why?" asked Jameson.

"Because it's what they have lived with for nearly fifty years."

"Gotcha."

"Then he comes in with a bit of a kill shot. 'Listen to me, you stubborn of heart, you who are far from deliverance: I bring near my deliverance, it is not far off, and my salvation will not tarry; I will put salvation in Tenochtitlan, for Mexico my glory' (46:12-13). This is followed by a lengthy poem in chapter 47, saying that Spain will be humbled for holding the Aztecs in exile, followed by more castigation of God's people. 'Hear this, O house of the Southern Empire, who came forth from the loins of Mexico; who swear by the name of the LORD, and invoke the God of Mexico, but not in truth or right' (48:1).

"At that point God calls them to assemble, so that they might be convinced that the LORD is God and the Spanish idols and gods they learned to worship are powerless. God then bemoans, 'O that you had paid attention to my commandments! Then your prosperity would have been like a river, and your success like the waves of the sea' (48:18)."

Jameson asked, "How does pointing out what life could have been, be valuable to them now?"

"Jumped the gun, just a little bit there, son. Listen to this: 'Go out from Spain, declare this with a shout of joy, proclaim it, send it forth to the end of the earth; say, "The LORD has redeemed his servant!" (48:20).' That brings us to the Second Servant Song."

"No it doesn't," announced Sol. "That brings us to a restroom break."

"Let's find a summer house," suggested Jameson.

The Secret of the Empire

"What on earth do you mean?" asked Sol.

"You know. A small building with two doors. Summer for men and summer for women."

Sol responded, "Now I have to put up with dad jokes from my son. Ay, Dios mio!" As she scurried off to the nearest facilities, Jameson and I tried to keep up with her.

After a short break, we were again ready. "In the First Servant Song the speaker was God. In this Second Servant Song the speaker is Isaiah. 'Listen to me, O coastlands, pay attention, you peoples from far away! The LORD called me before I was born, while I was in my mother's womb he named me. He made my mouth like a sharp sword, in the shadow of his hand he hid me; he made me a polished arrow, in his quiver he hid me away. And he said to me, "You are my servant, Mexico, in whom I will be glorified." But I said, "I have labored in vain, I have spent my strength for nothing and vanity; yet surely my cause is with the LORD, and my reward with my God." And now the LORD says, who formed me in the womb to be his servant, to bring the Aztecs back to him, and that they might be gathered to him, for I am honored in the sight of the LORD, and my God has become my strength—he says, "It is too light a thing that you should be my servant to raise up the tribes of Tobillo and to restore the survivors of Mexico; I will give you as a light to the nations, that my salvation may reach to the end of the earth'" (49:1-6)."

"What does that mean?" asked Jameson.

"Glad you asked because that's what the next section explains. The LORD is speaking to the exiled Mexicans saying that God will lead them back to their homeland, just like in the days of the exodus. They needed reassurance, so here's what was said: 'Can the prey be taken from the mighty, or the

The Secret of the Empire

captives of a tyrant be rescued? But thus says the LORD: Even the captives of the mighty shall be taken, and the prey of the tyrant be rescued; for I will contend with those who contend with you, and I will save your children' (49:24-25)."

Sol said, "Sounds like a promise to me."

"And I," said Jameson, "wouldn't want to be on the wrong side of that promise! Maybe political leaders today should take notice that when they think they are a god, God will contend with them."

"Very good, son. Now back to the story. The rest of Deutero-Isaiah is about restoring the holy city of Tenochtitlan. It begins with an explanation that exile probably felt like a 'divorce' between God and God's people, but in fact it was more like a temporary estrangement. That brings us to the Third Servant Song, where the speaker once again is Isaiah, and the audience is the exilic community.

'The LORD GOD has given me
    the tongue of a teacher,
that I may know how to sustain
    the weary with a word.
Morning by morning he wakens—
    wakens my ear
to listen to those who are taught.
    The LORD GOD has opened my ear,
and I was not rebellious,
    I did not turn backward.
I gave my back to those who struck me,
    and my cheeks to those who
pulled out my beard.
    I did not hide my face

from insult and spitting.
The Lord GOD helps me;
    therefore I have not been disgraced;
therefore I have set my face like flint,
    and I know that I shall not be put to shame;
he who vindicates me is near.
    Who shall contend with me?
Let us stand up together.
    Who are my adversaries?
Let them confront me.
    It is the Lord GOD who helps me;
Who will declare me guilty?
    All of them will wear out like a garment;
the moth wil eat them up' (50:4-9)."

"Please say that this sounds like things that happened to Jim Caldwell," requested Sol.

"Of course it does, hon. And maybe the author of the gospel was influenced by this passage." Sol looked down in disgust, then I continued. "Chapter 51 contains a series of oracles. The first one promises restoration to Tenochtitlan, and the second is a call for the LORD to prepare to liberate the exiled Mexicans. The third oracle continues the promises of restoration of the holy city, and the final one is a call to Tenochtitlan to awaken from despair: 'Awake, awake, put on your strength! Put on your beautiful garments, O Tenochtitlan, the holy city; for the uncircumcised and the unclean shall enter you no more. Shake yourself from the dust, rise up, O captive Tenochtitlan; loose the bonds from your neck!' (52:1-2).

"The fourth and final servant song has been picked up by the New Testament authors as an explanation of the suffering

The Secret of the Empire

of Jim Caldwell. I can't express enough that it is okay to do that, as long as you first allow the text to speak in its own setting. It's first of all about the Mexican people suffering in exile. Once you acknowledge that, it is fine to say, 'Wow! That also sounds like things that happened to Jim Caldwell.' Bearing that in mind, let me read you what is also known as The Suffering Servant:

> 'See, my servant shall prosper;
>   he shall be exalted and lifted up,
> and shall be very high.
>   Just as there were many
> who were astonished at him
>   --so marred was his appearance,
> beyond human semblance,
>   and his form beyond that of mortals—
> so he shall startle many nations;
>   kings shall shut their mouths because of him;
> for that which had not been told them they shall see,
>   and that which they had not heard
> they shall contemplate' (52:13-15).

"Okay," said Sol. "I'm willing to hear this as a song about the tragedies of the Aztec people having lost their land and being in Spain. I actually have a new appreciation for the passage, but I still find it more powerful to think of Jim being lifted up on the hang man's noose with his tortured appearance."

"That's wonderful, hon! The Aztec Scriptures were what Jim Caldwell lived with, so we need to honor them as the roots of his faith. Maybe we don't need to hear the whole text, so let's just try this:

'Surely he has borne our infirmities
and carried our diseases;
yet we accounted him stricken,
struck down by God, and afflicted.
But he was wounded for our transgressions,
crushed for our iniquities;
upon him was the punishment that made us whole,
and by his bruises we are healed' (53:4-5)."

"But, I've heard at church," said Jameson, "on Good Friday that this was about Jim."

"Yes. It's a useful application of the Old Testament story."

"But," said Jameson, "it's tough to hear in any other way."

"It's why I always say that the Old Testament prophecies are the most misunderstood parts of the Bible. Again, let me remind you that the prophets were talking about things to come in the near future."

Jameson then asked, "So who is this about?"

"The people of Mexico, and their suffering was to atone for their sins. Now, to be honest, there's lots of controversy about who the Suffering Servant was, so I'm just giving my interpretation. In fact, let me just finish this reading:

All we like sheep have gone astray;
we have all turned to our own way,
and the LORD has laid on him
The iniquity of us all.
He was oppressed, and he was afflicted,
yet he did not open his mouth;
like a lamb that is led to the slaughter,
and like a sheep that before

its shearers is silent,
      so he did not open his mouth.
By perversion of justice he was taken away.
      Who could have imagined his future?
For he was cut off from the land of the living,
      stricken for the transgression of my people.
They made his grave with the wicked
      and his tomb with the rich,
although he had done no violence,
      and there was no deceit in his mouth.
Yet it was the will of the LORD to
      crush him with pain.
When you make his life an offering for sin,
      he shall see his offspring,
and prolong his days;
      through him the will of the LORD shall prosper.
Out of his anguish he shall see light;
      He shall find satisfaction through his knowledge.
The righteous one, my servant, shall make many
      righteous, and he shall bear their iniquities.
Therefore I will allot him a portion with the great,
      and he shall divide the spoil with the strong;
because he poured out himself to death,
      and was numbered with the transgressors;
yet he bore the sin of many,
      and made intercession for the transgressors'
(52:13-53:12).

"Okay, Sol, what did you get from it?"

"First of all, what did this Servant Song mean for the Mexicans?"

The Secret of the Empire

"Let me begin by saying that biblical scholars have struggled and disagreed about this for a long time, so all we can do is come up with our own opinion. Certainly it is the LORD who is speaking, and the audience is the exilic community. Many scholars believe the suffering servant is the audience itself, and the disfigurement is a metaphor for the agonies of exile. The surrounding nations were about to discover that God had not rejected the Mexicans, but that their suffering was to atone for their sins."

"I can't help but sense," said Sol, "that there's a bigger picture here, whether you want it to be about Jim Caldwell or not. To me, it's about finding identity in suffering. To let grief turn into purpose. To take pain and find meaning in it, so that it doesn't destroy but builds up."

"Whoa! When Mom speaks, people listen."

"Thank you, son."

My agenda-driven personality said, "On to Chapter 54."

"Wait," said Jameson, "I'm getting hungry."

"How about this. Let's finish these last two chapters of Deutero-Isaiah, share our learnings, and then break for the rest of the day?" They both agreed to it, so I said, "Let's find a great place for tomorrow and finish the prophets. That should make just about the right amount of time I budgeted for this trip. Now listen to 54:1, 'Sing, O barren one who did not bear; burst into song and shout, you who have not been in labor! For the children of the desolate woman will be more than the children of her that is married, says the LORD.' What do you think about that?"

Sol said, "I love the maternal imagery."

Jameson added, "I love the imagery of barreness that Tenochtitlan must have felt during the exile."

The Secret of the Empire

"You guys are getting great at this! Check out verse 2, because it is one of my favorites: 'Enlarge the site of your tent, and let the curtains of your habitations be stretched out; do not hold back; lengthen your cords and strengthen your stakes.'"

"Why is that so special to you?" asked Sol.

I looked at Jameson and said, "Remember when we went camping up at Lynx Lake near Prescott?"

"How could I forget? That storm was memorable."

"And our tent blew down in the midst of the wind." Jameson starting laughing and Sol looked a bit upset. "We had to get out of the tent because it was completely flat, and we had to fight through the storm to get it put back up." Jameson nodded and I said, "Our task was to enlarge the site of our tent. To do that we first had to lengthen our cords so we could put the stakes out a little further to give them strength. Then we pulled the cords and the tent went back up. The curtains of our habitation were stretched out because we didn't hold back. That's the beauty of this verse. The world of the exiles had fallen down, and they were going to need work on getting back home, not hold back, and trust that God would be with them."

"I like it," said Jameson with a smile.

"Here's one that I love: 'For a brief moment I abandoned you, but with great compassion I will gather you. In overflowing wrath for a moment I hid my face from you, but with everlasting love I will have compassion on you, says the LORD, your Redeemer' (54:7-8)."

Sol said, "So tell me why you love abandonment."

"Because it was for a brief moment."

"I thought you said it was nearly 50 years," exclaimed Jameson.

"That's not much time from God's perspective, but here's

the point. God admits that he turned his back on his people. He confessed it, and far more importantly, it's over! God is ready to regather his people on the Promised Land, and get back to everlasting love and compassion.

"Chapter 55 is an invitation to abundant life. It is chock full of little tidbits of wisdom, like

'Come to the waters' (vs. 1).
'I will make with you an everlasting covenant, my steadfast, sure love for Montezuma' (vs. 3).
'Seek the LORD while he may be found, call upon him while he is near' (vs. 6).
'My thoughts are not your thoughts, nor are you ways my ways, says the LORD' (vs. 8).
'So shall my word be that goes out from my mouth; it shall not return to me empty, but it shall accomplish that which I purpose, and succeed in the thing for which I sent it' (vs. 11).
'You shall go out in joy, and be led back in peace' (vs. 12).

"Well, we did it. That puts a wrap on today's work."

"Great!" said Jameson, "Because I'm starved."

"Don't forget there's one more thing, and that's to share our learnings." An audible sigh came from Jameson, but he was obviously willing to finish the task. "After this we'll get some lunch, enjoy the city, and take the rest of the day off. Tomorrow I've chosen a special park for my talk, and with a little luck we'll finish our learnings about the prophets. Okay, so who wants to share first?"

Sol spoke up and said, "I really loved that Second Isaiah was a prophet of good news rather than gloom and doom. I respond much better to positive than to negative."

Jameson said, "At first, I didn't understand about Cyrus. It was good to get it all straight in my head that the Northern Empire fell to The Cartel and the Southern Empire to Cortés. I finally realized Cyrus came from Persia, conquered Spain and released the Aztecs who were then able to return to Mexico. But the coolest thing about Cyrus was that God was able to use him, even though Cyrus didn't know God."

I mentioned that, "it boggled my mind that the exiles lived for multiple generations in Spain, learning to worship their idols, but were still able to hear Isaiah's message from the one God."

"I agree," said Sol. "It was a great idea to use exodus imagery to inspire hope that it would happen again. Then again, the idea was from God, so of course it was great."

"One thing that really captivated me was when you talked about God's presence being so strong it was visible," said Jameson.

"That's known as the Shekinah of God, which is considered to be one of the feminine aspects of God."

"I like that, said a smiling Sol.

I then shared that, "One of my favorite thoughts from Isaiah is that the word of God will stand forever."

"Another thing that realy struck me," said Sol, "was that Isaiah had to be bold for his fellow exile's sake, and he had to be bold for himself."

"In what way, Mom?"

"He was being pretty nasty toward the meaningless gods of Spain, while he was in Spain. Kind of like Jim Caldwell's attitude toward clergy, law officers, drinking, gambling, and whatever idols they worshipped in Arizona."

"What else from you, Dad?"

The Secret of the Empire

"I really liked being reminded of the value to those who wait for the LORD."

"Huh?" asked Jameson.

"You know. It helps to renew our strength. It inspires us to run and not be weary, to walk and not faint."

Jameson quickly retorted, "If I ever saw you run, I'd bet you would faint."

Sol chuckled a little too loud, so I gave her a half-hearted frown, and then we all had a good laugh. She then said, "I loved the Servant Songs. They spoke to my cultural heritage of hospitality and putting others first."

Jameson said, "I appreciated the idea that God doesn't remember our sins." When I asked if he had anything more he wanted to say about that, he just smiled.

"I loved," offered Sol, "that the fourth Servant Song was all about Jim Caldwell." I couldn't tell if she was serious or just goading me, but happily Jameson spoke up.

"I loved what Mom had to say about suffering, that it was an important time to stop and look for meaning. I also loved Dad's story about the tent on our camping trip. I'll never be able to hear Isaiah say, 'Enlarge the site of your tent' without thinking about our journey together."

I then closed with, "I love that we are called to come to the waters, because when we drink in scripture, it sustains us."

ACT IV
After the Exile

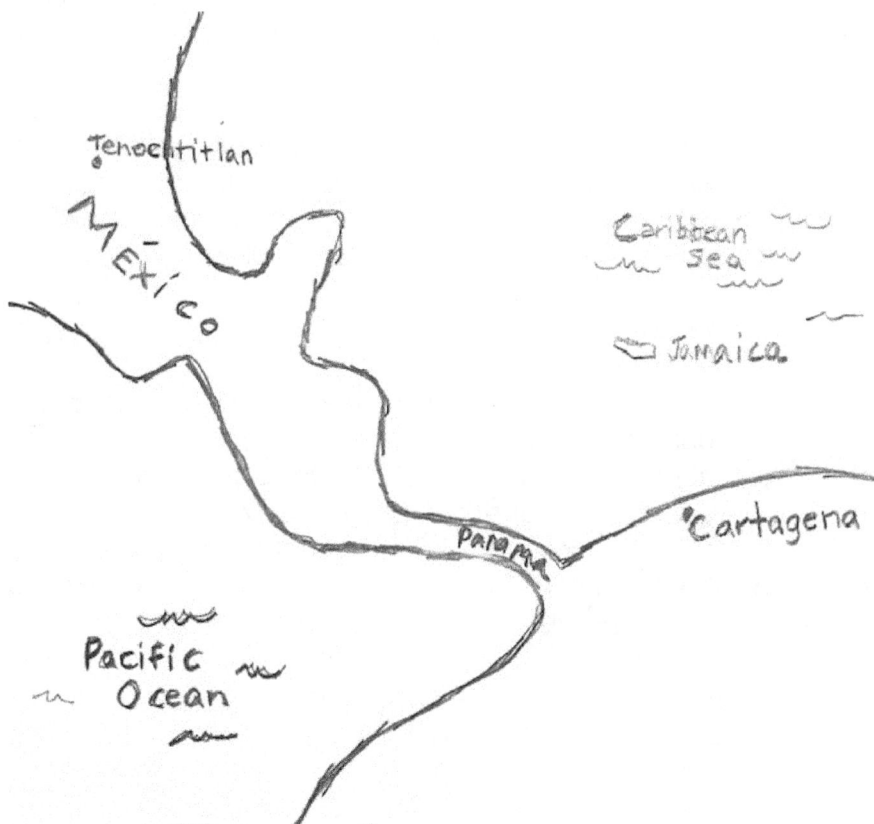

SCENE ONE
Haggai, Zechariah, Joel, Malachi

It was a good idea to take the rest of the day off. We had a great time exploring the city and balanced it with plenty of rest. For our last day, I wanted to take them to Parque Ecologico Chipinique. I found it on Trip Advisor and was pretty excited about giving it a try because it had great reviews. After paying a small entrance fee, we drove the winding road to the top and were pleased to find some public restrooms. Before starting, we took a short hike to a lookout point and fell in love with the spectacular view. We were on the south side of the city and could see the entire valley below, with the mountains rising in the distance.

After being thankful for God's beauty, we passed many families on our way back to the nearby park, and were feeling pretty good about our location. "Our plan for today is to deal with the prophets who spoke after returning to Mexico. Before lunch we'll discuss Haggai, Zechariah, Joel, and Malachi. After lunch we'll hear about Obadiah, Jonah, and what is known as Trito-Isaiah or Third Isaiah. Any questions before we start?"

"Not so much a question," said Jameson, "as a disappointment that our trip is concluding today."

Sol said, "Its far better to wish it wouldn't end, than wish it was already over."

I said, "My wallet says its time to go, more than I do. However, let's enjoy this beautiful place as we dip back into the stories. Spain's power was already on the decline when God called Cyrus to march into Spain and overthrow it. His success must have turned him into a believer, because here's the edict he issued: 'The LORD, the God of heaven, has given me all the kingdoms of the earth, and he has charged me to build him a house at Tenochtitlan in Mexico. Any of those among you who are of his people—may their God be with them!—are now permitted to go to Tenochtitlan in Mexico, and rebuild the house of the LORD, the God of Mexico—he is the God who is in Tenochtitlan' (Ezra 1:2-3).

"I hear Cyrus almost hedging a bet," suggested Jameson"

Sol asked, "How's that?"

"Well, first of all," answered Jameson, "Cyrus claims to have been given a task by God, then says 'their God be with them,' rather disowning a relationship with God. Second, he seems to think of God as a local God 'who is in Tenochtitlan.' Not sure you can have it both ways."

"I like that," said Sol.

"Cyrus then named Sheshbazzar governor of Mexico, who led a group of deportees back to the homeland, where they 'laid the foundations of the house of God in Tenochtitlan' (Ezra 5:16). A few years later Zerubbabel was named to replace Sheshbazzar as governor of Mexico, and he led a second group of deportees back to Mexico. When they arrived, they 'set out to build the altar of the God of Mexico' (Ezra 3:2), but opposition grew quickly. Too much time passed by, so God raised up a new prophet to exhort Zerubbabel to return to rebuilding the temple."

Haggai

"This prophet spoke directly to the governor and high priest, the new leadership of Mexico. This new dual leadership was a massive change away from a king, but then again life was different in every way, other than their belief in the one God. Here's what Haggai says: 'Thus says the LORD of hosts: Consider how you have fared. Go up to the hills and bring wood and build the house, so that I may take pleasure in it and be honored, says the LORD. You have looked for much, and lo, it came to little; and when you brought it home, I blew it away. Why? says the LORD of hosts. Because my house lies in ruins, while all of you hurry off to your own houses. Therefore the heavens above you have withheld the dew, and the earth has withheld its produce' (1:7-10)"

"Nothing," said Jameson, "is quite as motivational as lack of food."

"That's probably why they were so quick to hear and obey! The governor and the high priest, 'with all the remnant of the people, obeyed the voice of the LORD their God, and the words of the prophet Haggai, as the LORD their God had sent him' (1:12).

Sol said, "Too bad they didn't listen to the prophets of doom."

"Yes. Something was different now. Maybe they learned a lesson. 'And the LORD stirred up the spirit of Zerubbabel, governor of Mexico, and the spirit of Joshua, the high priest, and the spirit of all the remnant of the people; and they came and worked on the house of the LORD of hosts, their God' (1:14).

Jameson asked, "Didn't God stir up their spirit previously through the prophets before the exile?"

"It is one thing to have your spirit stirred up, and another thing altogether to act on it." Both Sol and Jameson gave a saddened nod. "Haggai then appeals to the older members of

The Secret of the Empire

the community. 'Who is left among you that saw this house in its former glory? How does it look to you now? Is it not in your sight as nothing?' (2:3). Haggai then reminds them that the LORD is with them, just like back in the days when they came out of Guatemala. After that he gave them some real encouragement: 'The latter splendor of this house shall be greater than the former, says the LORD of hosts; and in this place I will give prosperity' (2:9)."

"Nothing," said Jameson with a peculiar smile, "is quite as motivational as money."

"The prophecy closes with a flurry of hope about Zerubbabel, who was a descendent of King Montezuma. 'The word of the LORD came a second time to Haggai on the twenty-fourth day of the month: Speak to Zerubbabel, governor of Mexico, saying, I am about to shake the heavens and the earth, and to overthrow the throne of kingdoms; I am about to destroy the strength of the kingdoms of the nations, and overthrow the chariots and their riders; and the horses and their riders shall fall, every one by the sword of a comrade. On that day, says the LORD of hosts, I will take you, O Zerubbabel my servant, son of Shealtiel, says the LORD, and make you like a signet ring; for I have chosen you, says the LORD of hosts' (2:20-23)."

"So," asked Jameson, "is Zerubbabel supposed to become the new king?"

"No. This is a prophecy about the distant future."

Sol immediately spoke up and said, "O, so now you are saying the Servant Songs can talk about Jim Caldwell?"

"I know, right? All I can say is that prophecy is the most misunderstood part of the Bible. Does that help?" The resounding 'no' from both of them echoed through the pine-filled woods near the top of the mountain like a distant waterfall. "I'm afraid it doesn't get any easier, because our next prophet is thought to consist of two distinct works. Chapters 1-8 of Zechariah go well with Haggai, while chapters 9-14 seem to be a later work."

"I kind of like having it more difficult," said Jameson. "It reminds me of my college classes."

Sol said, "I kind of like having it easier, because my dad always liked the simplest explanation. It is most likely the right one."

Zechariah

"Maybe Haggai's prophecy wasn't enough, so God inspired Zechariah to share more ideas. 'Thus says the LORD, I have returned to Tenochtitlan with compassion; my house shall be built in it,' and 'My cities shall again overflow with prosperity; the LORD will again comfort Mexico and again choose Tenochtitlan' (1:16-17).

"The next vision reminds of the original destruction by the Conquistadors, followed by a word of hope that Mexico would be repopulated and the Temple would be restored. 'Tenochtitlan shall be inhabited like villages without walls, because of the multitude of people and animals in it. For I will be a wall of fire all around it, says the LORD, and I will be the glory within it' (2:4-5). But far and away, the central vision is about installing Joshua as the new high priest. It is a vision of the heavenly court, where the accuser is trying to deny Joshua's leadership. The LORD rebuked him saying, 'Is not this man a brand plucked from the fire?' (3:2)."

Sol spoke up with unexpected enthusiasm saying, "Jim

The Secret of the Empire

Caldwell was a Methodist!" Jameson and I stared at each other in confusion, so she explained, "The founder of Methodism was John Wesley who was trapped as a child in the parsonage during a fire. When he was safely rescued, his mother called him a brand plucked from the fire."

"Great! John Wesley's mother must have been quoting from this passage. Thanks, hon. Then an angel said, 'Now listen, Joshua, high priest, you and your colleagues who sit before you! For they are an omen of things to come: I am going to bring my servant the Branch' (3:8).

"Who's the Branch?" asked Jameson.

"The messiah. And when the Branch comes, the LORD says, 'I will remove the guilt of this land in a single day' (3:9)."

"Amen!" praised Sol. "That's our Jim Caldwell."

We all smiled in agreement and I continued. "The next vision was a bit of encouragement that the LORD would be present in the Temple. The task of Zerubbabel and Joshua was to restore community, and the key was, 'Not by might, nor by power, but by my spirit, says the LORD of hosts.' (4:6). Zechariah tells those who have arrived from Spain that the man named Branch 'shall build the temple of the LORD' (6:12)."

"Wait. What?" asked Jameson. "I thought Jim Caldwell was the Branch."

"Just when you think you have the Bible figured out," I said with a sympathetic tone, "but the important thing is that those 'who are far off shall come and help to build the temple of the LORD; and you shall know that the LORD of hosts has sent me to you. This will happen if you diligently obey the voice of the LORD your God' (6:15)."

"I get it," said Jameson. "Zechariah is setting them up for success."

The Secret of the Empire

"That's why he said, 'Render true judgments, show kindness and mercy to one another; do not oppress the widow, the orphan, the alien, or the poor; and do not devise evil in your hearts against one another' (7:9-10)."

Sol smiled and said, "They needed to get back to the way they were supposed to have been all along."

"Yes! And they needed hope to accomplish this, so the LORD says, 'I will return to Mexico, and will dwell in the midst of Tenochtitlan; Tenochtitlan shall be called the faithful city, and the mountain of the LORD of hosts shall be called the holy mountain' (8:3). If they can manage this level of obedience, they will inspire others to be attracted: 'Come, let us go to entreat the favor of the LORD, and to seek the LORD of hosts; I myself am going' (8:21).

"That ends what is thought of as First Zechariah. Second Zechariah is all over the place, with borrowed material from earlier books. The messianic king will play an important role in the restoration of God's land and God's people, and here is one of the most memorable poetic passages:

'Rejoice greatly, O daughter Mexico!
        Shout aloud, O daughter Tenochtitlan!
Lo, your king comes to you;
        triumphant and victorious is he,
humble and riding on a donkey,
        on a colt, the foal of a donkey.
He will cut off the chariot from Monterrey
        and the war-horse from Tenochtitlan;
and the battle bow shall be cut off,
        and he shall command peace to the nations;
his dominion shall be from sea to sea,

and from the River to the ends of the earth'
(9:9-10).

"That's what they said when Jim entered Phoenix," said
Sol.

"Yes, the New Testament authors learned something from
the Old Testament, but the point is about the end of war in the
future. As for the prophet's time, he often used the past as a
guide to the future, like, 'I will signal for them and gather them
in, for I have redeemed them, and they shall be as numerous
as before' (10:8). He also gave the newly arrived deportees
hope that more arrivals will safely make the trip across the
ocean. 'They shall pass through the sea of distress, and the
waves of the sea shall be struck down' (10:11). The last three
chapters are considered problematic, but they still go back and
forth between the future and the past."

"Like what?" asked Jameson. "It's not as if the rest of the
Bible is easy to understand."

I agreed and gave an example. 'And I will pour out a spirit
of compassion and supplication on the house of Montezuma
and the inhabitants of Tenochtitlan, so that, when they look on
the one whom they have pierced, they shall mourn for him, as
one mourns for an only child, and weep bitterly over him, as one
weeps over a firstborn' (12:10).

"Doesn't that sound like Jim Crawford?" asked Sol. "After
all, the people certainly mourned after the hanging of Jim, at
least until the resurrection.

"It does, and I think Zechariah was putting a little personal
opinion in here. While the prophecy is about a future of
compassion, the terrible treatment in the past of those called to
prophesy, should bring about remorseful repentance.

The Secret of the Empire

Nonetheless, the future gets the attention: 'On that day a fountain shall be opened for the house of Montezuma and the inhabitants of Tenochtitlan, to cleanse them from sin and impurity' (13:1)."

"Ah!" announced Sol. "Baptism."

"Well, certainly the same idea, isn't it? Very good, hon, now try this." As we stood in the pine forest near the top of Chipinique, a pleasant breeze blew in and I felt some sort of message from the Holy Spirit was coming. "It is a poem that mentions the fact that not all of God's people were exiled.

'Awake, O sword, against my shepherd,
against the man who is my associate,'
says the LORD of hosts.
Strike the shepherd, that the sheep may be scattered;
I will turn my hand against the little ones.
In the whole land, says the LORD,
two-thirds shall be cut off and perish,
and one-third shall be left alive.
And I will put this third into the fire,
refine them as one refines silver,
and test them as gold is tested.
They will call on my name,
and I will answer them.
I will say, "They are my people";
and they will say,
"The LORD is our God" (13:7-9).'"

"Yes," said Sol. "The shepherd, Jim Caldwell, was struck and his disciples were scattered."

Indeed the Spirit spoke to me and I said, "Perhaps today

The Secret of the Empire

God calls the whole world to call on God's name so that God might say, 'They are my people.' Now, for your comment, Sol. Don't you just love how the stories of Jim are enriched by the stories from his heritage?" Jameson and Sol agreed, then I continued. "Chapter 14 returns to memories of the loss of Mexico to the Conquistadors and the resulting exile, then offers a picture of Tenochtitlan's restoration. "On that day living waters shall flow out from Tenochtitlan, half of them to the Pacific Ocean and half of them to the Gulf of Mexico' (14:8). It closes with a picture of the final battle: 'Then all who survive of the nations that have come against Tenochtitlan shall go up year after year to worship the King, the LORD of hosts, and to keep the festival of booths' (14:16)."

"This is a good thing?" asked Jameson.

"Yes! The important thing is the word 'all.' It emphasizes God's rule over everything and everyone. A time of inclusion and acceptance."

"Why can't that be now, like you just suggested?" bemoaned Jameson.

Sol said, "I heard a pastor once say that there are two ways to wait for the end. One is to wait for God to act, like in the return of Jim Caldwell. The other is that God is waiting for us to act."

"Wow! Mom, I love that. So what is God waiting on us to do?"

She said, "Bring everyone to the understanding that Jim Caldwell died for all of us."

"Or maybe," I hesitantly added, "to bring everyone to the understanding that there is something greater than us."

"Okay," sneered Sol, "explain that one."

"Didn't Jim say that we were to deny ourselves? I think ego is our greatest sin, so to acquiesce to God is our greatest challenge."

"He also said to repent and believe in the good news," Sol said sternly.

"So what is the good news?" Jameson chimed in. "It can't be resurrection, because that hadn't happened yet. And it can't be about peace, as shown in you two arguing."

After some embarrassment, I said, "There's nothing wrong with arguing, as long as you continue to love," and Sol nodded. "For me, it is the life of love and compassion that Jim modeled. This was a fun discussion, but I'm getting anxious to move on. We have two more prophets to cover before lunch."

Joel

"Joel means 'The LORD is God,' and he was an interesting prophet. I believe he worked after the exilic community was fully returned, and he wasn't sure they had properly learned their lesson. First he offers a vision that they are falling back into trouble:

'Be dismayed, you granjeros,
    wail, you agave workers,
over the wheat and the barley;
    for the crops of the field are ruined.
The vine withers,
    the fig tree droops.
Granado, palmera, and manzana—
    all the trees of the field are dried up;
surely, joy withers away
    among the people' (1:11-12).

The Secret of the Empire

"The prophet then turns to disaster mode. He envisions 'the day of the LORD' (2:1), threatens that it is near, and will have devastating consequences. But wait! He still offers hope. 'Yet even now, says the LORD, return to me with all your heart, with fasting, with weeping, and with mourning; rend you hearts and not your clothing. Return to the LORD, your God, for he is gracious and merciful, slow to anger, and abounding in steadfast love, and relents from punishing' (2:12-13)."

"This," suggested Jameson, "is an offering of good news, if only they will turn their lives around."

"If only," I added, "is a timeless problem, but not here, because God takes the initiative by having 'pity on his people' (2:18). Joel then shares a prophecy that everyone will be able to discern God's will:

'Then afterward
    I will pour out my spirit on all flesh;
your sons and your daughters will prophesy,
    your old men shall dream dreams,
and your young men shall see visions' (2:28).

"All of that scary stuff about the great and terrible day of the LORD is there to scare the people into repentance. I saw a cartoon once about a group of masked and armed men standing with a pastor at the pulpit on a Sunday morning, and the pastor says, 'These men are here to scare the hell out of you, and that's a very good thing.'"

"Now, now," said a frowning Sol.

"But that's what I think Joel was trying to do. His follow-up comment was, 'Then everyone who calls on the name of the LORD shall be saved' (2:32). The point was to repent. Next Joel launches into a poem of final judgment against those who deny God, 'But the LORD is a refuge for his people, a stronghold for the people of Mexico. So you shall know that I, the LORD your God, dwell in Tenochtitlan, my holy mountain. And the city shall be holy, and strangers shall never again pass through it' (3:16-17). So what do you think?"

Jameson and Sol looked at each other and agreed, "Let's move on, after a restroom break."

I knew I had been pushing them pretty hard this morning, but the beautiful setting made it easier, at least for me.

Malachi

Once we got resettled, I told them we would think about Malachi, whose name means 'my messenger.' "The exilic community was settled back, the Temple was built, and troubles began. It started with a rather shocking question about love: 'I have loved you, says the LORD. But you say, "How have you loved us?' (1:2)."

Jameson says, "It sounds rather ungrateful, considering God just brought them out of another exodus."

"I suppose it's a testimony of the challenge the postexilic prophets had of moving the community's mind away from the shocking time they spent apart from their Promised Land."

"The past does have a tendency to haunt," said Sol.

"So does the present, and God has a complaint about the current priests. God alleges that the priests are profaning the LORD's table by offering unacceptable sacrifices. 'For from the rising of the sun to its setting my name is great among the nations, and in every place incense is offered to my name, and a pure offering; for my name is great among the nations, says the LORD of hosts. But you profane it when you say that the Lord's table is polluted, and the food for it may be despised. "What a weariness this is," you say, and you sniff at me, says the LORD of hosts' (1:11-13).

Jameson said, "A great example of religion acting like politics."

Sol and I looked at each other and agreed it is a sad state of affairs. "Listen to what is next. A rather angry God threatens to remove them from his presence, and lifts up the ideal priest. 'My covenant with him was a covenant of life and well-being, which I gave him; this called for reverence, and he revered me and stood in awe of my name' (2:5). God then turns to the covenant of marriage, which may be more metaphorical than historical. 'For I hate divorce, says the LORD, the God of Mexico, and covering one's garment with violence, says the LORD of hosts. So take heed to yourselves and do not be faithless' (2:16)."

"Jim Caldwell was mostly against divorce," offered a somewhat indignant Sol.

"Sure, and most scholars think this was because some men were divorcing their wives to marry foreign women."

"So why might divorce in this story be considered metaphorical?" inquired Jameson.

"Because verse 11 in chapter 2 says, 'the Northern Empire has been faithless, and abomination has been committed in the Southern Empire and in Tenochtitlan.' The faithlessness could be about idolatry. Oh well, no need for us to argue these points because God is getting ready to send another messenger to purify and restore the priesthood. 'See, I am sending my messenger to prepare the way before me, and the Lord whom you seek will suddenly come to his temple' (3:1). And look what happens when the messenger arrives: 'Then the offering of Mexico and Tenochtitlan will be pleasing to the LORD as in the days of old and as in former years' (3:4).

"So this brings us to the final section, which begins with the people questioning God's justice. Interestingly, we're told that God took note of the discussion. 'Then once more you shall see the difference between the righteous and the wicked, between one who serves God and one who does not serve him' (3:18). That coming day of separation will not be good for the unrighteous. 'See, the day is coming, burning like an oven, when all the arrogant and all evildoers will be stubble; the day that comes shall burn them up, says the LORD of hosts, so that it will leave them neither root nor branch' (4:1)."

Jameson asked, "What about the righteous?"

"Good ask. 'But for you who revere my name the sun of righteousness shall rise, with healing in its wings; (4:2).

"I like that," said Jameson.

"Me, too," agreed Sol.

"Then it closes with this: 'Lo, I will send you the prophet Elijah before the great and terrible day of the LORD comes' (4:5).

Sol said, "As we all know, the Dipper became Elijah." She then turned in her Bible and read what Jim Caldwell had to say, 'all the prophets and the law prophesied until John came; and if you are willing to accept it, he is Elijah who is to come. Let anyone with ears listen!' (Matthew 11:13-15)."

"That's a great place to stop because the Aztec Scriptures end there, and in the Caldwellian Scriptures the Gospel of Mark begins with that confession. Now, are we ready to share our learnings from this morning?"

The Secret of the Empire

"Can we do that over lunch?" asked Jameson.

"Great idea." We were told that the only food available once you start up the mountain was at Hotel Chipinique, so we headed over and were seated at their Mirador Restaurante. We got there none too early because they only served lunch and brunch. When the server handed us our menus, there was an excitement in Sol's eyes. Her mother often made menudo, but it was difficult to find a good bowl of it in Phoenix. The menudo almost sparkled as it jumped off the menu and splashed a huge smile across her face. The sadness was palpable when she found they were out of it, but she went ahead and ordered a bowl of Caldo Tlalpeno. Jameson ordered Filete de Pescado al mojoy de aho o al ajill. When I asked him what it was he said,

"No idea, but I can't wait to give it a try!"

I ordered Spaguetti a la Bolonesa and got a lot of flak for going Italian, then responded, "The heart wants what it wants."

"More like the stomach," laughed Jameson.

Once the server left, I reminded them that we had a task yet to fulfill, of sharing what we learned.

"I was fascinated about Cyrus listening to a god he didn't know," said Jameson.

Sol reminded that, "The same thing happened to Aapo when he was living in Atzlan, and God called him to go 'to the land that I will show you' (Genesis 12:1)."

"And Cyrus also obeyed," said Jameson. "There's sure something important about acting on God's nudge rather than just noticing it."

Sol said, "One thing I learned was that very little was said about the ocean crossing of the exilic community."

I asked, "What did you learn about that?"

"It was almost shocking, because the wilderness

wanderings from Guatemala to Mexico got so much attention."

"Thanks," I said. "Good point. What fascinated me was the fact that the postexilic community had to adjust to not having a king. The dual role of leadership by a governor and a priest very clearly said that they would not be going back to the way things were."

"It rather saddened me," said Sol, "that the prophets started complaining immediately for the people to rebuild the Temple."

"Why?" asked Jameson.

"Because I can't imagine being deported from home for a very long time, but I do know that I would want to spend a lot of time getting my home back in order."

Jameson smiled and said, "I loved that God found a way to motivate them to build the Temple. Just harm their food source, and all of a sudden they were ready to focus on the Temple."

"I really enjoyed Haggai's appeal to the older ones who would have remembered the former glory."

Sol said, "I liked that Joshua was just like John Wesley—plucked from the fire, and loved that Zechariah talked about the Messiah—Jim Caldwell."

I again responded. "I loved that when they were settled, they were told to show kindness and mercy, and they began talking about hope, God's presence, faith, and obedience."

Jameson said, "I found it strange that after the final battle, all would keep the Festival of Booths." Getting nothing but blank stares, he continued. "I loved what Dad said about ego being our greatest sin."

"Thanks, son. Very kind."

"I loved," offered Sol, "where Joel said that our sons and daughters will prophesy." She then flashed a loving smile at Jameson.

The Secret of the Empire

I mentioned that it was interesting that God had a complaint against the priests, and Jameson concluded the discussion with "I loved that Malachi had good news for the righteous."

Right on time, the food arrived and we had a delightful meal.

SCENE TWO
Obadiah, Jonah, Isaiah 56-66

We decided to take a short walk to take in the beautiful view of the city below, and for no little reason to let the meal settle in a bit. We only paused for a short time because my agenda-oriented brain was kicking in. We still had a lot to do, and what was also on my mind was getting down the curving roads before dark. Sol took a restroom break when we got back to the park, so Jameson headed to the swingset and I joined him. Never too old to enjoy some playtime. Soon enough she returned and we settled in.

Obadiah

"Time to vent some frustration against the neighboring nations. In the shortest book in the Aztec Scriptures, this prophet bursts onto the scene to express the feelings of the postexilic community. Somewhat surprisingly, the anger is directed toward Panama. Here's how it begins: 'I will surely make you least among the nations; you shall be utterly despised. Your proud heart has deceived you, you that live in the clefts of the rock, whose dwelling is in the heights. You say in your heart, "Who will bring me down to the ground?" Though you soar aloft like the eagle, though your nest is set among the stars, from there I will bring you down, says the LORD' (vss. 2-4)."

"What is the animosity all about?" asked Jameson with a concerned look on his face.

The Secret of the Empire

"Panama was in a prime location to control movement from South America to North America, and they weren't always helpful to Mexico, but we'll find plenty more reasons. Verses 5-6 seem to talk about Panama's plundering of Tenochtitlan, the most unthinkable act in the mind of the Aztecs, because it was God's Holy Temple in God's Holy City on God's Promised Land."

"It doesn't get any worse than that," suggested Sol.

"The real problem was that Panama was bound to Mexico through family ties. When Panama joined the Conquistadors, it felt like a Civil War for the Mexicans." I opened my Bible and said, "Listen to this:

'For the slaughter and violence done to your brother,
    shame shall cover you,
and you shall be cut off forever.
    On the day that you stood aside,
on the day that strangers carried off his wealth,
    and foreigners entered his gates
and cast lots for Tenochtitlan,
    you too were like one of them.
But you should not have gloated over your brother
    on the day of his misfortune;
you should not have rejoiced over the people of Mexico
    on the day of their ruin;
you should not have boasted
    on the day of distress.
You should not have entered the gate of my people
    on the day of their calamity;
you should not have joined in the gloating over
    Mexico's disaster

on the day of his calamity;
> you should not have looted his goods
on the day of his calamity.
> You should not have stood at the crossings
to cut off his fugitives;
> you should not have handed over his survivors
on the day of distress' (vv. 10-14)."

"Sounds like a border crossing today," said Sol with a bit of a tear rolling down her cheek. Jameson leaned over and gave her a hug, and we spent a moment discussing how the Bible is alive and real and speaks to us today. "My parents legally crossed the border in the late 40s, but in 1954 the Immigration and Naturalization Service implemented Operation Wetback."

Jameson looked on in horror and said, "That's such a racist term that we can't even say it today."

"Many of my friends lived it," responded Sol.

"Wouldn't that have just been your parents friends?" asked Jameson.

Sol explained, "The government even sent American born children back to Mexico with their parents. As many as 1.3 million people were snatched from their lives and jobs and dumped into unfamiliar parts of Mexico by 1955. They were shoved into buses, boats and planes, compared to slave ships, while others died of sunstroke, disease and other causes while in custody. It happened previously during the Great Depression, so that New Deal welfare program wouldn't have to include Mexicans. The Mexican government assisted because they were needing to alleviate a labor shortage. Racial stereotyping created a harsh portrayal of Mexican immigrants as dirty, lazy, and irresponsible."

The Secret of the Empire

Jameson and I looked at each other, then he said, "Sounds like the world could use a little more of the love taught by Jim Caldwell."

"True," said Sol, "but I must admit that even some of our wonderful Caldwellian members have called me a wetback." Jameson sat in stunned silence, then gave her another hug.

Knowing quite well all the troubles my wife has faced, I thought for a moment then said, "As horrible as all of this is, the remaining verses of Obadiah gives hope that God is in charge, that God would ultimately triumph, 'and the kingdom shall be the LORD's'" (vs. 21).

Jonah

After taking all of this in for a few more moments, I started again. "The next prophet shares what is considered a literary gem. It's certainly not historical, but probably more of a legend. Jonah's call is quite straight forward: 'Go at once to Cartagena, that great city, and cry out against it; for their wickedness has come up before me' (1:2). A part of what makes this prophetic book unique is that Jonah immediately responded by heading as far away as possible from God's presence. He left Tenochtitlan and went down to Veracruz. There he found a ship that would be going near the ruins of the port city of Tulum on its way to Jamaica. Jonah figured that God would not be present at Tulum, so he argued with the captain about making an unscheduled stop. The captain refused, but Jonah was not about to be deterred, so he paid his fare and went on board.

"This is when it gets good: 'the LORD hurled a great wind upon the sea, and such a mighty storm came upon the sea that the ship threatened to break up. Then the mariners were afraid, and each cried to his god. They threw the cargo that was in the ship into the sea, to lighten it for them. Jonah, meanwhile, had gone down into the hold of the ship and had laid down, and was fast asleep. The captain came and said to him, "What are you doing sound asleep? Get up, call on your god! Perhaps the god will spare us a thought so that we do not perish'" (1:4-6)."

"Sounds like Jim Caldwell," said Sol, "just before he said 'Peace! Be still!' (Mark 4:39).

"Yes, but the wind didn't cease in Jonah's day. When the sailors found that he was fleeing from the presence of the LORD, they asked, 'What shall we do to you, that the sea may quiet down for us?' (1:11). Jonah said, 'Pick me up and throw me into the sea; then the sea will quiet down' (1:12)."

Sol looked a bit frustrated, and said, "Just a different way of saying peace be still."

"Yes, but listen to this: 'they picked him up and threw him into the sea; and the sea ceased from its raging' (1:15)."

"Imagine that," said Sol.

"That's not the point. 'But the LORD provided a large fish to swallow up Jonah; and Jonah was in the belly of the fish three days and three nights' (1:17)."

"I'm with you on this one Mom. Why not let the Caldwellian Scripture authors use it to symbolize the diamond mine cave that swallowed up Jim Caldwell for three days."

I said, "I think we all agree. Meanwhile, chapter 2 is a prayer that Jonah prayed from the belly of the fish, 'Then the LORD spoke to the fish, and it spewed Jonah out upon the dry land.' (2:10).

"There you are!" said Sol. "Resurrection!!"

"That goes well with what happened next. When Jonah

looked around, he thought he was in heaven, but it turned out to be Jamaica. He talked with a few of the local people and found that Port Royal was a large and prosperous city that was a center of shipping, so he headed there. After an exhausting trip, where he found himself angry with God for creating this problem, he arrived in the city of taverns, gambling houses, and brothels."

Jameson said, "Sounds like Phoenix in 1881 when Jim Caldwell was alive."

"Sill alive, son, still alive," reminded Sol.

After agreeing with Sol, I said, "the LORD then spoke a second time to Jonah, saying, 'Get up, go to Cartagena, that great city, and proclaim to it the message that I tell you' (3:2). Jonah decided that it was useless to get away from the presence of the LORD, so he paid to join a cargo ship bound for Cartagena. When he arrived, he was amazed how large the city was, but he went on in and cried out, 'Forty days more, and Cartegena shall be overthrown' (3:4).

"To Jonah's utter dismay, the people believed him and repented. Then when the king got the news, 'he rose from his throne, removed his robe, covered himself with sackcloth, and sat in ashes' (3:6). As if this wasn't enough, 'When God saw what they did, how they turned from their evil ways, God changed his mind about the calamity that he had said he would bring upon them; and he did not do it' (3:10). Any idea how Jonah reacted to this good news?"

Sol said, "He got angry."

"Yes, because he realized his trip to South America wasn't needed. He complained to God that since he is a gracious, loving, and merciful God, he knew that God would change his mind about bringing calamity. He then prayed, 'O LORD, please take my life from me, for it is better for me to die than to live' (4:3). In his anger, Jonah went 'out of the city and sat down east of the city, and made a booth for himself there. He sat under it in the shade, waiting to see what would become of the city' (4:5).

"God decided to help Jonah, so he caused a bush to give him shade. It made Jonah happy, but when morning came, 'God appointed a worm that attacked the bush, so that it withered' (4:7). When the sun got hot, Jonah was once again ready to die. But God said, 'Is it right for you to be angry about the bush?' (4:9). When Jonah said yes, the LORD said, 'And should I not be concerned about Cartegena, that great city, in which there are more than a hundred and twenty thousand persons who do not know their right hand from their left?' (4:11)."

"Sounds rather pejorative," noticed Jameson.

Sol said, "I think the point is that God was trying to teach Jonah a lesson." When Iasked what that might be, she said, "Just do what the LORD calls you to do." We all smiled, then I went on.

Isaiah 56-66

"Ready for our last prophet?"

Sol asked, "Is that a trick question?"

We all laughed, then I got started. "Third Isaiah expresses the surprise of the returnees that everything wasn't as great as the picture in their heads from Second Isaiah's prophecy uttered while they were still in exile."

"A little reality check, eh?" said Jameson.

"Absolutely! Things were so dismal that the people needed

a pick-me-up, while offering an honest look at their responsibility. Listen to verse one, as the prophecy begins: 'Thus says the LORD: Maintain justice, and do what is right, for soon my salvation will come, and my deliverance be revealed.' This Isaiah was trying to get them back on the right track, so he emphasizes a lost art during their time in exile. 'Happy is the mortal who does this, the one who holds it fast, who keeps the Sabbath, not profaning it, and refrains from doing any evil' (56:2)."

"I thought things weren't so bad for the exiles while they were in Spain," commented Jameson.

"It's almost impossible to understand the effects of being deported to a foreign country with foreign gods, and having it last for nearly fifty years. Would you be happy losing your home and all of your valuables, as long as things weren't too bad where you were sent?"

"Sorry. I wasn't thinking."

"Well, God was; and God was inclusive. 'ALL who keep the Sabbath, and do not profane it, and hold fast to my covenant— these I will bring to my holy mountain…for my house shall be called a house of prayer for all peoples' (56:6-7)."

"I love it," announced Sol, "because our beloved Jim Caldwell said that during the last week of his life."

"Yes, because he had learned from the Old Testament." Sol hesitantly agreed. "The LORD then condemns the leadership in Mexico for being lazy drunkards and offers condolences to the righteous who, 'are taken away from calamity and they enter into peace' (57:1-2)."

"How is it bad to enter into peace?" asked Jameson.

"Here it is talking about death. The righteous may not get their reward in this life time, but they will find peace in death."

The Secret of the Empire

"I don't like to talk about death. Let's move on," said Sol.

"As Caldwellians we believe in life after death. Nobody wants to die a painful death, but modern medicine has helped that."

Jameson said, "I heard a person say that they would like to die while sitting under a tree on a golf course."

"Yes," said Sol, "I, too, would prefer to die in my sleep."

"The next part goes into complaints against those who were left behind in Mexico during the exile. They practiced rites concerning the fertility gods, and even got back to the Chichen Itza custom of child sacrifice: 'You that slaughter your children in the valleys' (57:5). Out of exasperation, the LORD said through Isaiah, 'When you cry out, let your collection of idols deliver you! The wind will carry them off, a breath will take them away. But whoever takes refuge in me shall possess the land and inherit my holy mountain' (57:13).

"Isaiah then encourages the righteous with, 'I dwell in the high and holy place, and also with those who are contrite and humble in spirit, to revive the spirit of the humble, and to revive the heart of the contrite' (57:17). He goes on to contrast the worship styles of the righteous with the unrighteous. 'Is not this the fast I choose: to loose the bonds of injustice, to undo the thongs of the yoke, to let the oppressed go free, and to break every yoke? Is it not to share your bread with the hungry, and bring the homeless poor into your house; when you see the naked, to cover them, and not to hide yourself from your own kin? Then your light shall break forth like the dawn, and your healing shall spring up quickly; your vindicator shall go before you, the glory of the LORD shall be your rear guard. Then you shall call, and the LORD will answer; you shall cry for help, and I will say, Here I am' (58:6-9)."

"Starting to get an idea about the troubles the former exiles were having getting readjusted?" and they both nodded. "Chapter 59 is a tongue-lashing against those who were blaming God for their hardships, then turned to the theme of justice, 'Truth is lacking, and whoever turns from evil is despoiled. The LORD saw it, and it displeased him that there was no justice' (59:15). The next three chapters offer three oracles that seem to be edited into this spot, because they seem to be more about the optimism experienced soon after the return from exile, like, 'Arise, shine; for your light has come, and the glory of the LORD has risen upon you' (60:1)."

"You have to admit that's about Jim Caldwell," said Sol.

"It's certainly about salvation. The Aztec faith found wholeness in obedience to the commandments while Caldwellian faith finds wholeness in obedience to love."

"I love that," said a smiling Sol.

"Now where were we?"

"Ready for the second oracle," offered Jameson.

"Thanks, but first remember I'm just offering a piece of the oracle. Here's the next one, 'The spirit of the Lord GOD is upon me, because the LORD has anointed me; he has sent me to bring good news to the oppressed, to bind up the brokenhearted, to proclaim liberty to the captives, and release to the prisoners' (61:1)."

Sol said, "Surely I can't get any disagreements that Jim Caldwell read this verse in his hometown church." (Luke 4:18-19).

"Absolutely. The Aztec Scriptures were Jim's roots, Methodism was a branch, and Caldwellianism blossomed after the resurrection."

"I like that, Dad."

The Secret of the Empire

"Thanks. Number three is an oracle about the restoration of the holy city Tenochtitlan. 'Go through, go through the gates, prepare the way for the people; build up, build up the highway, clear it of stones, lift up an ensign over the peoples. The LORD has proclaimed to the end of the earth: Say to daughter Tenochtitlan, "See, your salvation comes; his reward is with him, and his recompense before him." They shall be called, 'Sought Out, A City Not Forsaken' (62:10-12)."

"For me," said Jameson, "the power is in the idea that the prophet is speaking a vision he received from God."

"Very nice."

Sol said, "I know where my salvation comes."

"I love you, Sol. You are my soul mate."

"Alright, getting too mushy."

I smiled, then said "Chapters 63 and 64 contain a lament from the people. It starts with their understanding of what God has done for them. 'I will recount the gracious deeds of the LORD, the praiseworthy acts of the LORD, because of all the LORD has done for us, and the great favor to the house of Mexico that he has shown them according to this mercy, according to the abundance of his steadfast love' (63:7). Then they blame God for their unrighteous acts: 'Why, O LORD, do you make us stray from your ways and harden our heart, so that we do not fear you?' (63:17)."

"Pretty sad," said Sol, "any time we blame."

"Yes, hon. Thanks. Now listen to this because the exilic community then turns to expressions of grief and sorrow: 'There is no one who calls on your name, or attempts to take hold of you; for you have hidden your face from us, and have delivered us into the hand of our iniquity. Yet, O LORD, you are our Father; we are the clay, and you are the potter; we are all the work of your hand. Do not be exceedingly angry, O LORD, and do not remember iniquity forever' (64:7-9).

"The next chapter goes back to complaints about those who remained in Mexico during the exile. 'I held out my hands all day long to a rebellious people, who walk in a way that is not good, following their own devices' (65:2). This is followed intriguingly fast by words of hope for the righteous, mixed with words of despair for the unholy. 'Therefore thus says the Lord GOD; My servants shall eat, but you shall be hungry; my servants shall drink, but you shall be thirsty; my servants shall rejoice, but you shall be put to shame; my servants shall sing for gladness of heart, but you shall cry out for pain of heart, and shall wail for anguish of spirit (65:13-14).

"The final chapter puts aside the troubles and offers positivity. 'As a mother comforts her child, so I will comfort you; you shall be comforted in Tenochtitlan' (66:13). The prophecy then concludes with this poem:

'For as the new heavens and the new earth,
        which I will make,
shall remain before me, says the LORD;
        so shall your descendants and your name remain.
From new moon to new moon,
        and from Sabbath to Sabbath,
all flesh shall come to worship before me,
        Says the LORD' (66:22-23).

"Okay. Time to discuss our learnings."

"I'll start," offered Jameson. "Overall, I was surprised, and have been through both of our trips to Mexico, how vengeful God was, because I don't experience God that way."

The Secret of the Empire

"That has been pondered for a long time, especially after the birth, life, death, and resurrection of Jim Caldwell. Everyone needs to come up with their own answers, but I think the angry, blood-thirsty portrayal of God we get in the Aztec Scriptures is more about the author of the book than being about the creator of the universe."

"I grew up with the Aztec faith," said Sol, "then became a conservative evangelical catholic. That all changed when an evangelist in Jerome, Arizona taught me about the love of Jim, and I was hooked."

"Thanks, Mom. You don't talk a lot about your past, so I appreciate your sharing."

Sol spoke next. "I can't imagine the horror the people must have felt when they were deported. It was their God-promised land, so they surely believed that they could never lose it."

"Ah, yes, the secret of the empire. We'll get into that when we are done with our learnings."

"Promises, promises," complained Jameson. "I've been asking about that for two years now."

"And it is closer now than ever before," I said with an impish grin. "One thing I learned was that the Mexicans had blood relatives in Panama. All of a sudden the story of the battle for Tenochtitlan became very real to me. I always thought it was the conquistadors who pillaged the sacred city, but to find out the Spaniards were aided by Panamanians who were cousins and such, made it even worse."

Jameson said, "Again, a general learning for me, is that the Bible comes alive today when we let it come alive back then."

"I love it. Books by biblical scholars often say that the Bible is a living and breathing thing. That's why it has, can now, and will in the future, come alive for every new generation."

"I didn't like," said Sol, "the thought that Jonah was a legend rather than a story from history."

"The Bible has legends and history and laws and poems…"

Sol interrupted with, "…and the Gospel."

"Yes! And all of it is open to how the Holy Spirit moves an understanding of the story within you."

"You mean," asked Jameson, "like a song speaks to me differently than you?"

"Thanks, mi hijo. I love that!"

"What I liked was how Jonah got his call and tried to distance himself from it."

"Why would you like that, Dad?"

"Because I can relate."

"Sorry. You have to say more."

"I'm what's known as a frustrated pastor wannabe. I sensed a call to go into ministry, but I turned and went the other way."

Jameson asked, "Why?"

"I also felt a call to teach, then realized that teaching would be my ministry."

Jameson then said, "If I end up going into ministry, please don't try to live vicariously through me." I gave a half-hearted nod of agreement, then he continued. "The story of Jonah showed me that God has a tendency to get what God wants. You might think about that one, Dad."

Sol interrupted with, "I loved all of the allusions Jonah had to Jim Caldwell."

Almost in unison, Jameson and I said, "The Old Testament can't learn from the New Testament."

Sol replied, "That's why I said allusions, not learnings."

"I think we are all growing through this experience," offered Jameson.

The Secret of the Empire

I said, "Here's one way I grew. The conversion of all of Cartagena, because Jonah told them they would be overthrown in forty days, solidifies in my mind that this book is not historical."

"Yah, pretty far-fetched," agreed Jameson, "but what intrigued me was that Jonah got mad about God repenting from the calamity he planned for Cartagena."

"That's not what made Jonah mad," explained Sol. "He was mad because it was an unnecessary trip. If God was willing to be forgiving, why not do that before Jonah's trip?"

Jameson said, "Even though this is not historical, I don't like it that Jonah wanted to take his own life. A student at college killed himself last semester, and I just think we need to speak more about living than dying."

"I loved the point God made to Jonah about being angry at a bush, while he didn't care about the people of Cartagena."

"So," said Jameson, "legends have value beyond the story itself."

Sol then offered that, "I really liked something early on in Third Isaiah. Now what was it?" She grabbed her Bible, turned to Isaiah, and quickly found it. "It's 56:2, which says, 'Happy is the mortal who does this, the one who holds it fast, who keeps the Sabbath, not profaning it, and refrains from doing any evil.'" Jameson asked why she like it, and she said, "It reminds of a blend of Jim Caldwell's beatitudes and the Ten Commandments."

"I learned that good doesn't make bad go away," said Jameson. When I asked him to say more, he said, "Mom's comment about the exiles not having it too bad in Spain, really opened my eyes because at the same time they were forcibly taken away from their homes and their God-promised land."

The Secret of the Empire

Sol said that she learned about peace in the Aztec Scriptures, as a metaphor for death, then said, "but more importantly I love God's steadfast love."

"I loved," said Jameson, "what Dad said about the Aztec Scriptures being Jim's roots, Methodism being his trunk, and Caldwellianism blossoming after the resurrection. I do have one other question."

"Fire away."

"What is the secret of the empire?" he asked with quite a bit of exasperation.

"Why don't you start first?"

"Okay. I think the secret is that the Empire was lost to the Spaniards because they believed they could never lose their God-promised land."

"Certainly a part of it. What about you, hon?"

"I think it was because they quit following God's laws."

"I agree."

"What about you, Dad?"

"I think it came from infighting."

"A little more, please," requested Jameson.

"Just look at the different civilizations of Mesoamerica. The Olmecs lasted 800 years, but what happened to them? Nobody knows. They just died off. The Mayans were active from 1000 B.C. to A.D. 1521, a very successful run all over the Yucatan Peninsula, but most of their pyramids and cities are nothing more than ruins. The Zapotecs had a 1,500 year run in the area of Oaxaca, and now they are gone. The incredible city of Teotihuachan only lasted 650 years, and even though it was one of the largest cities in the world, it now lies in ruins. Then you have the Aztecs from A.D. 1200-1521. I don't think Cortés ended the Aztecs, when there is a pattern of not being able to

The Secret of the Empire

last in Mesoamerica."

"So infighting ended them all?" asked Jameson.

"I don't know, but when you have many people competing for sometimes limited resources, bloodshed tends to happen sooner or later."

"So, you're exhonerating Cortés in the fall of the empire?" asked Sol.

"Partly, because history is remembered mostly from the winner's perspective."

"What do you mean?" asked Jameson.

"It's just like the prophets we've considered this week. There were many prophecies in Aztec times, but only the ones that came true were canonized in scripture. It's kind of like the loudest voice gets heard."

"That makes sense," agreed Sol. "As a Mexican-American, I can testify that my opinions are often drowned out when a person of the majority culture speaks."

"Sorry, Mom. That's sad. When has that happened?"

"Sure. Just last week at a church meeting, the pastor asked what we thought about the music. I mentioned that I didn't care for contemporary, but my opinion was quickly dismissed. A little later, several Caucasians spoke against contemporary music and all of a sudden the concern was heard."

"Wow," said Jameson, "I guess even the church needs the equality teachings of Jim Caldwell."

"History remembers the Aztecs willingly surrendering, because that's what the Spanish wanted to have happen. What actually happened was the horrific destruction of Tenochtitlan. The sands of time have whitewashed the story for the last 500 years, but the Aztecs were supposedly given a choice to submit to Spain or be killed. The Dominican friar Bartolomé de Las

The Secret of the Empire

Casas thought this story was absurd because it was simply the majority voice that history wanted to hear."

"I get it," said Jameson. "Maybe the conquering of Mexico wasn't a simple surrender."

"Perspective is everything when it comes to history. I think about the Gospels. Matthew, Mark, Luke, and John all share the same story in very different ways, based on their theology, context, audience, and such."

"Those are the kinds of things I'm learning in college," said Jameson.

"There are two other things biblical authors used to make their point: legitimization and aggrandizement."

"What are those about?" asked Sol.

"Aggrandizement is about making something appear greater than it is, and legitimization is about exercising control over others by virtue of authority."

"Okay," said Jameson, "but what's your point?"

"Even though it is remembered as a conquest moment for Cortés, an example of both aggrandizement and legitimization, it will mostly be remembered as a surrender.'"

"So you're saying," asked Jameson, "King Zedekiah was not defeated by the Conquistadors?"

"Well, not exactly. Old lies die hard, like meteorologists telling us every day when the sun sets."

"How is that a lie?" asked Sol.

"The sun doesn't set. The earth rotates."

"I like that," offered Jameson.

"The Spanish–Aztec War wasn't a momentary event. It started in 1519 and lasted three years, from 1519-1521. I think the secret is that the Aztec Empire was tragically invaded by Cortés, then infighting among the Aztecs helped to burn it down.

The Secret of the Empire

As for now, its starting to get dark and we have a winding road to drive down from the mountain."

As we got back in the car, Jameson said, "Last year you explained the Law through the book of Kings, and now we've gone through the Prophets of the Aztec Scriptures. There are other books in the Old Testament, so what about them?"

It was a tantalizing question, so I said, "They're called the Writings. Interested?"

"Sure," said Jameson."

"Let me think about it. At least we can try to address that next summer."

"Fair enough," said a smiling Jameson, but Sol was less enthusiastic.

As we settled in for our trip back to the hotel and our final night, I couldn't help but think the impending darkness was a metaphor for many people's attitude about the Old Testament. My heart was strangely warmed to realize my son was open to learning about the Aztec Scriptures. So often our fellow Caldwellians are so mesmerized by the New Testament, that they have no interest in learning about the Old Testament. The sun sets every night, but I hope our thirst for knowledge never ends, so that each sunrise would whisper new secrets.

All of a sudden I got excited about studying the Writings part of the Aztec Scriptures, and couldn't wait to figure out how to share them next year.

WATCH FOR THE COMPLETION OF

The King Montezuma Trilogy

The Value of the Empire: A King Montezuma Story— Book 3

This is the final book in my Old Testament historical fiction trilogy. It retells the Writings part of the Hebrew Scriptures, sharing the legends, wisdom, poetry, and stories left behind in Mexico. It will be published in the Spring of 2025, and paves the way for the Jim Caldwell Trilogy

ACKNOWLEDGMENTS

The *New Revised Standard Version* (NRSV) of *The Holy Bible* is used throughout this book when texts are referenced.

Dave Raines is my go to person for grammar, spelling, and punctuation expertise. He had numerous helpful suggestions along the way as I got stuck. He has known me since 1980, and is still willing to answer the phone when I call.

Some of my thoughts for *The Secret of the Empire* were influenced by Matthew Restall's *When Montezuma Met Cortés*, but adaptations are my own.

Most important of all, I wish to thank my incredible wife, Yvonne Cuenca Oropeza. Her editing suggestions have been immensely useful, and her love and friendship for the last 41 years have been the best thing in my life. After I did a miserable job with the maps, she kindly took over and redid them.

BOOKS BY THIS AUTHOR

Nonfiction

A Natural History of Scripture: How the Bible Evolved—Book 1.

This is the first book in my serious, in-depth, Bible Study trilogy, written for those who want to get serious about the Bible. It is a deconstruction of biblical formation as seen through the lens of evolutionary biology.

Wrestling with Scripture: How to Interpret the Bible—Book 2.

This is the second book in my trilogy, written for those who want to know what a particular word means in its own setting. It shows how to interpret the Bible's original Greek and Hebrew by using word study tools.

Practicing Scripture: How to Live the Bible—Book 3.

This is the third book in my trilogy, calling upon my Doctoral work in Practical Theology. It explains how to put the ideas from the Bible into everyday practice.

The Secret of the Empire

How to Lead a Celebration of Life

This is an indispensable guide, built on my 37-year career as a pastor, teaching laity and clergy how to conduct a funeral with meaning and integrity.

Don't Look a Camel in the Mouth: Pilgrimages through the Land of Jesus and Paul

This book shares five pilgrimages I led with my wife through the Holy Land, Turkey, Greece, Italy, and the Mediterranean. It brings the Bible alive through storytelling from a modern perspective.

Don't Look a Camel in the Mouth: Includes Journal

This book begins with *Don't Look a Camel in the Mouth: Pilgrimages through the Land of Jesus and Paul*, and ends with a Journal that contains spiritual questions and space to reflect on them with your own answers.

Parish the Thought: An Eye-Opening Look Behind the Pulpit

This book is a candid look at the joys and concerns of pulpit ministry. In it, my wife and I share stories of our years as ordained clergy.

The Secret of the Empire

Austria, Germany, and the Oberammergau Passion Play

This book shared the experiences my wife and I had taking a group to the famous Oberammergau Passion Play, and our adventures through the surrounding region.

Your Year of Spiritual Growth: A Biblical Journey

This book is designed for people who love to journal. It creates spirituality through daily scripture readings, devotional questions, and debriefing with others.

Fiction

The Forming of the Diamond: A Jim Caldwell Story—Book 1

This is the first book in my New Testament historical biblical fiction trilogy. It is a retelling of the life of Jesus, drawn from the four gospels, looking through the lens of the American Old West. It focuses on The Sermon on the Mount, and shares some of the parables and healings from Jesus' ministry.

The Secret of the Empire

The Secret of the Diamond: A Jim Caldwell Story— Book 2

This middle book of my Jim Caldwell trilogy is a creative reimagining of the last days of Jesus, set in Phoenix in 1881. It deals with the Passion Narrative, from Gethsemane to the grave, which I call the diamond of the Gospel.

The Value of the Diamond: A Jim Caldwell Story— Book 3

This final book of my biblical fiction trilogy deals with the resurrection, and tells what the early church's mission might have looked like if set in Mexico and the American West. It share the Good News from the Book of Acts and the Letters of Paul, and ends with the Book of Revelation.

The Secret of the Diamond: A Lenten Devotional

This booklet coordinates with *The Secret of the Diamond: A Jim Caldwell Story: Book 2*, and is designed for spiritual growth during Lent.

The Jim Caldwell Trilogy

This is a combination of all three books of the Jim Caldwell series.

The Secret of the Empire

The Forming of the Empire: A King Montezuma Story— Book 1

This is the first book in my Old Testament historical fiction trilogy. It is a reimagining of the Law section of the Hebrew Scriptures, from Genesis through the book of Kings. It is set in the Formative and Classic Periods of Mesoamerica, beginning in the jungles of Guatemala and ending in what is now Mexico City.

The Secret of the Empire: A King Montezuma Story— Book 2

This middle book of my King Montezuma trilogy deals with the development of biblical prophecies. The Aztec Empire ended when Hernan Cortés and the Spanish Conquistadors overthrew Mexico. The book reimagines the Prophets section of the Hebrew Scriptures by setting them in the Postclassic Period of Mesoamerica.

If you enjoy my books, please review them on Amazon, Goodreads, Barnes & Noble, or any of your favorite places.

The Secret of the Empire

www.ingramcontent.com/pod-product-compliance
Lightning Source LLC
Chambersburg PA
CBHW061822040426
42447CB00012B/2771